Walking the High Ridge

THE *CREDO* SERIES

A *credo* is a statement of belief, an assertion of deep conviction. The *Credo* series offers contemporary American writers whose work emphasizes the natural world and the human community the opportunity to discuss their essential goals, concerns, and practices. Each volume presents an individual writer's *credo*, his or her investigation of what it means to write about human experience and society in the context of the more-than-human world, as well as a biographical profile and complete bibliography of the author's published work. The *Credo* series offers some of our best writers an opportunity to speak to the fluid and subtle issues of rapidly changing technology, social structure, and environmental conditions.

Walking the High Ridge

LIFE AS FIELD TRIP

Robert Michael Pyle

Scott Slovic, *Credo* Series Editor

Credo

MILKWEED EDITIONS

Published 2000 by Milkweed Editions
Printed in Canada
Cover illustration by Geoff Du Feu/Masterfile
Front-cover design by Big Fish; spine and back-cover design by Sarah Purdy
Photographs of author by Thea Linnaea Pyle
The text of this book is set in Stone Serif.
00 01 02 03 04   5 4 3 2 1
First Edition

Milkweed Editions, a nonprofit publisher, gratefully acknowledges support from
our World As Home Funders: Lila-Wallace Reader's Digest Fund; Creation and
Presentation Programs of the National Endowment for the Arts; and Reader's
Legacy underwriter Elly Sturgis. Other support has been provided by the
Elmer L. and Eleanor J. Andersen Foundation; James Ford Bell Foundation;
Bush Foundation; General Mills Foundation; Honeywell Foundation; Jerome
Foundation; McKnight Foundation; Minnesota State Arts Board through an
appropriation by the Minnesota State Legislature; Norwest Foundation on
behalf of Norwest Bank Minnesota, Norwest Investment Management and
Trust, Lowry Hill, Norwest Investment Services, Inc.; Lawrence and Elizabeth
Ann O'Shaughnessy Charitable Income Trust in honor of Lawrence M.
O'Shaughnessy; Oswald Family Foundation; Ritz Foundation on behalf
of Mr. and Mrs. E. J. Phelps Jr.; John and Beverly Rollwagen Fund of the
Minneapolis Foundation; St. Paul Companies, Inc.; Star Tribune Foundation;
Dayton's, Mervyn's, and Target Stores by the Target Foundation; U.S. Bancorp
Piper Jaffray Foundation on behalf of U.S. Bancorp Piper Jaffray; and generous
individuals.

Library of Congress Cataloging-in-Publication Data

Pyle, Robert Michael.
    Walking the high ridge : life as field trip / Robert Michael Pyle.—1st ed.
        p. cm. — (Credo)
    Includes bibliographical references (p.).
    ISBN 1-57131-242-0 (pbk.) — ISBN 1-57131-243-9 (cloth)
        1. Pyle, Robert Michael. 2. Natural history—Authorship. 3. Naturalists—
United States—Biography. I. Title. II. Credo series (Minneapolis, Minn.)

QH31.P96 A3 2000
508'.092—dc21
[B]   00-035493

This book is printed on acid-free, recycled paper.

For Thea

Walking the High Ridge

Does there not exist a high ridge where the mountain-side of "scientific" knowledge joins the opposite slope of "artistic" imagination?

—Vladimir Nabokov

Walking the High Ridge

Walking the High Ridge

LIFE AS FIELD TRIP

by Robert Michael Pyle

A black butterfly roams the arctic-alpine heights of the Rocky Mountains. Its name is Magdalena, and I am never more alive than when I am up there with it.

For forty years, I have clambered up the ridges and rockslides where *Erebia magdalena* dwells, every chance I've had. I have caught it with a net and banged my knees and shins on countless boulders attempting to do so. I have watched it with binoculars for hours and photographed it, cryptic against black lichen and nectaring on pink moss campion like a lump of coal in a bed of roses. More times than I can remember, the clouds have closed just as I reached the habitat, sending me downslope again to outrun the summer lightning while the black butterflies retreated beneath the rocks.

All this time I have been trying, I guess, to catch not butterflies, but the living essence of one kind of life distilled from the highest, cleanest, most heartbreakingly fragrant landscape I know.

One summer, I tried to emulate the classic experiments of Niko Tinbergen, in an effort to learn about

3

Magdalena as a sexual being. Tinbergen, the teacher of Konrad Lorenz, had studied the courtship responses of male European grayling butterflies to both real females and artificial models of the species. He found that the males exhibited much more fervor when reacting to superfemale models. Magdalena alpines belong to the same subfamily as the grayling, known as the satyrs, and I was curious as to whether they would respond in the same way. I built a two-foot model Magdalena out of black photographic mounting board, with a wooden abdomen fitted with a metal ferrule. By running monofilament fishing line through the ferrule, I could "fly" the model—christened Maggie May—down the mountainside, and watch what happened.

Fortunately, I had a field assistant for other work that summer. Young David Shaw was willing—a few times—to carry Maggie May back up the steep rockslide above twelve thousand feet elevation at Loveland Pass in Colorado. But soon he tired of this, and I had to do it myself, while he stood at the bottom to try to catch the swarthy sailor before it crashed into the rocks.

The setting where Maggie flew was as stunning as ever. We left the springy, flowered tundra beside an alpine tarn whose shore smelled of every fishing trip I'd ever taken with my father—smells of mud, wet willow roots, worms, and the fish themselves. The boulderfall came down almost to the water, invading the tundra in the inbetween land called the fellfield. From there, the only thing was to climb, to scramble over the shining boulders, watching for loose rocks, for the giant orb webs that could catch your face, for the flickers of cinder and ash that meant the special butterflies of the talus: the rockslide checkerspot, the lustrous copper, the Melissa arctic, the Magdalena alpine.

The rocks stretched all the way up to the thin and brilliant blue above the ridge. When I judged we were high enough, I held one end of the line aloft from the end of my long net; the other was anchored far below. Then I launched Maggie May onto the almost empty air. Rolling a few degrees back and forth, she flew beautifully over the rocks, hundreds of feet down to a soft or hard landing, depending on the catcher's dexterity. Pikas, the gray brown boulder bunnies that call the rocks their own, first mounted their well-limed outposts to watch our progress; then, as the great black form sailed over, they dove into the boulder holes with a high-pitched, terrified "Geek!" For all they knew, Maggie was a raven, or worse.

And the Magdalenas? The males abandoned their cursory trajectories in midfloat, launched from their campion patches and basking stones, literally threw themselves at the passing shadow of superlative proportions. Whether out of an instinct to repel competing males or investigate potential females (they look alike), their response was dramatic and unequivocal. I would never again regard encounters between alpines as a random event: these black butterflies knew what they were doing. Back down in the mining town of

Georgetown in the Red Ram Tavern, I reread Herman Strecker's 1880 original description of *Erebia magdalena*, from the same vicinity; and I realized that what we'd learned about this dramatic animal in a hundred years could be put in one of its minute eggs, those fluted ovalettes that would be dropped among the alpine grasses after mating encounters more natural than the ones I had prompted with Maggie May.

Not everything I want to know about the black butterfly, as one emanation of the natural world, can be learned through the scientific approach. Some questions can be closed in on through experimentation and close, attentive observation. Others yield to the imagination, in concert with the colors, the smells, the cold crush of the stones and the soft lift of the high alpine air itself. Even before the summer of Maggie May, twenty-five years ago now, I began a novel that I am still honing through its eighth draft or so. *Magdalena Mountain* seeks a sense of this black beast, the stony world it inhabits, and the lives of the people it affects, through all the tools available to me as watcher and writer.

On the morning following the storm, Erebia crept up the damp walls of his nocturnal shelter, clinging to each granite grain with his tarsi, and emerged into a sunny morning. His receptors buzzed to the warm and perfectly polarized light of a cloudless sky. Several minutes of basking on his side against the black lichens warmed his flight muscles enough to work. As long as he lay there, he was cryptic against the surface. Then, at the moment his body reached the magic temperature, he launched into flight and became anything but invisible against the indigo sky.

He began halfway up the rockslide, which took in a portion of the southeast-facing slope below the north ridge of Magdalena Mountain. He flew directly upslope, toward the zenith. Upon reaching the ridge, he was swept up on a morning updraft, and might have dropped over the arête to the other side, except that it faced northwest and lay still in the clamp of the cold shadow. The sunshine bid him back to the east, whence it flowed.

So Erebia began, for the first time that day but perhaps the hundredth since emergence, his hang-gliding descent of the scree. Alert always for a black shape other than his own, he fell, flapped once, glided, flapped again several times slowly, and glided again, up-down-across, up-diagonal-down, until he reached the unfamiliar green of grass, prostrate juniper, and the first pines at the bottom of the slide: a ride of some three thousand vertical feet, but hardly direct, in twenty minutes. The ascent took longer and required more energy: Erebia paused twice to nectar and thrice to bask.

During that first flight, he encountered nothing but his own shadow, which diverted him briefly, as a kitten's tail will do when she has almost learned that it is attached. The next time, a randy Milbert's tortoiseshell took after him. Erebia circled once, perceived the fire-rimmed wing, and abandoned the encounter. On his third flight, curiosity over a water pipit might have got him in serious trouble had that bird not been sluggish after a meal of hellgrammites from a rivulet downslope. The fourth course brought interludes with two other *Magdalena* alpines, both male, and a *Melissa arctic*. With each one he do-si-doed on the wing. But these encounters gave no whiff of the scent that says female, no stimulus beyond the initial visual cue, and Erebia proceeded on his way.

It is good that in animals of poppyseed brains, hormones spring eternal, taking the place of hope. Never disillusioned, they simply try and try again. Or perhaps it is not so different with us. Were it not for hope and hormones, in whatever mix, many of us might retire to the flowerfields too soon; as surely Erebia would have done ere he found a female, had something ineffable and undeniable not driven him on, back up those rocks, once again to sail on down.

Biology doesn't mind a bachelor, for there tend to be too many males of most species; too many, that is, in view of the vast numbers of gametes each one is capable of producing. But nature abhors a spinster. Her eggs are far too precious to go rotting in her dying, virgin body; too precious, if survival is to keep apace of the losses. By contrast, in our own kind, our need is to limit our fecundity. The act of not reproducing becomes acceptable, helpful, even heroic. Among living species, only ours threatens to spoil its own estate through the sheer shoving of its numbers. Seldom have other species the need to lower their birthrates. Or if they do, reabsorption of the embryo, mass emigration, or starvation step in to sort things out. But as a rule, most creatures need all their femalekind mated, while the many redundant males can mate or not, for all nature cares, as long as the fitter ones get their innings. A garland draped around the loins of the females might suitably announce "Only the fit need apply."

So it is that female butterflies emerge later than the males, waiting until the numbers of potential mates have thinned themselves out, leaving the strong males alive. And then they mate rapidly: later encounters usually find females less than receptive. And without the omnipotent, ever present urge, many of the fittest survivors might just give up and never pass their genes.

But there is such a force. So the black butterfly (showing now more than a hint of brown plush in the right light) flew once again to the arête, where he found an inflorescence of a yellow mustard whose nectar he had never tasted before. As he sucked the sweet liquor his blood sugar rose, and he prepared to fly. Carefully he withdrew his drinking-straw proboscis from the nectary, recoiled it like a watch spring, preened it with his tiny brushlike forelegs, and tucked it between his furry labial palps. It was too valuable an implement to risk getting it stuck up with syrupy nectar, or otherwise damaged. Then, nourished, groomed, and warm, Erebia took off for his fifth descent of the day. If he could discriminate cumulus clouds from mountains, as he probably could, he might have felt a greater sense of urgency now. It was nearing noon. The clouds were rising, and the day was doomed. Scarcely an hour's worth of courting time remained.

Erebia scaled a huge boulder and alighted briefly on its top, surprising a pika that said, "Geek!" and sailed off again as the mammal dove for cover. Near the bottom of the boulder a pink patch of moss campion drew him down to drink again. But a more urgent vision took over as a dark smudge entered his broad, shortsighted field of view. He swerved to investigate.

The black form rose to meet him, and they circled one another jerkily. It was another Magdalena—but this time, a female. She glistened with the iridescence of a newly minted Erebia, shining purple and emerald like a violet green swallow, and her black held the depth of every night there ever was. She'd come out from her chrysalis only that morning, and scarcely a scale was missing from her wings. His antennae found her perfume on the alpine air, and Erebia smelled at last what he was born to find.

Erebia sensed something entirely new in his experience, as the female alpine's pheromones shivered his ganglia. With a fervor he'd never felt in the false flights of earlier encounters, he charged his carbon copy. Unreceptive before, she had repelled two other courtiers earlier that morning. Now, her wings dry and her own hormones flowing, she, too, felt a surge of urgency. The pair performed half a dozen pas des deux in an aerial ballet choreographed by centuries of selection, rising a dozen feet above the rocks. Close, but not touching, exchanging scents as intensity of purpose grew, the twin black shadows finally dropped together among the stones.

Quickly male and female circled one another in a

dance of recognition. So important—don't hybridize with the wrong kind, don't waste genes, don't blow your reason for living in this stony, bony land! Erebia palped the tip of his partner's body with his antennae, receiving a strong dose of her special scent. She stroked him with her own antennae—not his abdomen, but his forewings. There she found the thick, velvety patches of androconia, plush pads of sex scales wherein male satyrs' pheromones arise. Now there was no doubt. Magdalena scent, male and female, had flowed between them, following their private dance. No arctic, no other sort of alpine, could make this scent. There would be no mistake.

Like a series of locks and keys made smooth and slippery with graphite, the partners' sexual rhythms flowed together. They backed end-to-end on a rock, everting their swollen genitals. These sensitive tissues rubbed together for a second or two before Erebia's handlike claspers, gaping wide, found their way around the female's endpoint. In a reversal of the common pattern, she entered his body before he could enter hers. Then he closed around her so that, should they be forced to fly, she could carry his passive form without losing hold.

Feeling only Pan knows what, Erebia probed his aedeagus toward his mate's bursa copulatrix. Then, slowly, he passed his sperms to her, not in semen but parceled in a tidy packet called a spermatophore. There they would lodge until each egg, passing down from her ovaries, would receive the charge of life from Erebia's seed.

The act completed, a kind of gentle subsidence overtook the lovers—for may they not be called such? From first encounter through courtship to copulation lasted only a few minutes; the giving of the spermatophore took longer. Even after, the mates remained together.

Like one another's shadows, like an object and its reflection in a pool of ink, like a Rorshach test for a very calm mind, the two lay bonded. Like obsidian chips from a master point maker's nap, like paired punctuation marks inscribed on the tablet of the mountain's stone, like black valentines, they reposed. Erebia's wings enfolded between those of the larger female, her abdomen embraced within his body's clasp—such is butterfly love.

So they remained throughout the long mountain night, for a storm arose and sent them understone for shelter, still paired.

My heart lives high in the Colorado mountains, way up where the Magdalena alpine flies. But it also calls home the mossy damp precincts of the Northwest coast, where I live most of the time. Each year in the late winter, I travel down the Oregon shore to the Sitka Center for Art and Ecology for a writer's retreat, a deep immersion in work away from all the distractions of home. It is always my hope that this indwelling will let me plumb sinkholes I've never suspected in the porous strata of the imagination: the negative image, maybe, of what the expansive Colorado sky gives me; the soft shadow of the high ridge, a declivity of the mind where everything falls in together.

When my wife and partner, Thea, and I arrived last February, a welcome note awaited us from Randall Koch, the campus director. "Welcome back to Sitka," the message read. "The weather is suitable for working inside, although I hope, if you have a laptop, you have an adequate surge protector, given the rowdy activity outside."

Ran was right about the rowdy: Sitka spruce boughs whapped the windows of our snug holt, known as Russ's Tree House. Varied thrushes hunkered below, thrashing among the cones and bark chips. Bright kinglets flitted among them like the animated flecks of foam that dodged across Highway 101 anywhere it skirted the sea the previous day. The weather report on KLCC out of Eugene predicted gusts to seventy miles per hour on the headlands. We were perched just behind Cascade Head, one of the wildest and most jutting headlands on all of the Oregon coast. Rowdy wind we would surely have, and rain, though less than the two yards of it that had graced our own precincts three hours to the north over the past two months. And what we would *not* have was the telephone, the post, the piles of untended papers, and, gods save us, e-mail.

As for a stormsafe computer, I was in good shape. My laptop was a thick black ringed notebook, wide ruled. On the desk beside me sat a Sitka-made pot containing a yellow bouquet bright as any of van Gogh's sunflowers. The stems were a dozen-bunch of new number 2 Universal black lead pencils made in China—a glyphing technology little removed from the pencils both produced and employed by Henry Thoreau. Their shavings lay at the base of the pot like the frilly, shed petals of pinks; cedar spirals thin rimmed in ruffles of yellow paint. Actually, more the yellowy orange of a Union Pacific locomotive. The first ones sharpened were freshly washed, the later ones smudged gray like the UP tender behind the diesel engine stack. As I chiseled them to buffy, black-tipped cones, with a small implement of German steel, the graphite powdered out onto the six-sided stalks. When I finished, my fingers shone silver gray.

My equipment was rounded out by a couple of virginal Pink Pearl erasers manufactured in Malaysia; a box of candles, a box of firewood, a box of matches. Six bottles of Bridgeport India Pale Ale. And six whole days, that would come, no matter how hard the wind blew: a storm-proof writing system. And yes, I did have, in case it should be necessary, an adequate surge protector: it was the deliberate speed with which I can make words on paper with pencil. Because, though I have never suffered from writer's block, I have certainly been subject to the opposite. I could well imagine that I might need protection from the surge of words that such an invitation as Sitka's was likely to unleash.

My first time at Sitka, in January of 1997, I was also there with Thea. We read *Smilla's Sense of Snow* to each other in the window seat at night (except it was the British edition, *Miss Smilla's Feeling for Snow*), and by day I wrote an introduction to a book, and a short story. Afterward, we chased spring down the coast to camp among the dispersing monarch butterflies at Morro Bay. The next year I came alone for a short week. I read Penelope Lively novels in the evening, hacked at a great clot of overdue correspondence, and composed one poem. Now I'd come again with Thea, and we would read *Cold Mountain* as the wind shivered the giant spruces on either side of the cabin and the North Pacific surf hammered the shore below.

In the Tree House guest book, my friend and Sitka Center stalwart Kim Stafford, who initiated these winter residencies, wrote upon finishing his own previous retreat: "Completed #1 of 5 things I hoped to do, but that is one that would not otherwise be." This time, I had little idea what I would write. But whatever came out, it would be one thing that would not otherwise be and had never been before.

Driving up the entry lane to the Sitka Center the first night, we found a blacktail doe awaiting our arrival—or merely irritated by it, more likely. And then Thea, going to light a fire in the woodstove, rescued from the laid kindling a child's pencil-and-watercolor drawing of a buck standing erect in the woods—clipped off so that only one ear, one eye, one antler remained, but nicely rendered down to the delicate cloven hooves. The next morning I stepped outside, into the forest, among an infinitude of mosses and ferns. Tasting sleet from the crotches of the spruces, I looked up to see two little blacktails breaking trail for me. All week, the deer in the drive-way, the deer in the woodstove (posted beside my desk), and especially the deer in the forest, stayed with me. They reminded me of how I began to spiral in on the writing craft in the first place, to wrap the scalloped cedar skirts back into a whole, round and round, to a point. The deer took me back to a teacher who made all the difference.

A few years ago, giving a reading from *The Thunder Tree* at the Aurora History Center, a book that is set in Colorado, I was delighted to find my sixth-grade teacher from Peoria Elementary School in the audience. Doris Ferguson no longer had the sharp hearing that caught us out when my friends and I tried to put anything over on her, but her smile was the same. As we talked afterward, she told me that my fourth-grade teacher, whom I had heard was long gone, indeed still survived.

When I was next back in Denver, I went to see her at her home in Thornton. Maude Linstrom Frandsen (then Butler) was the definitive 1950s fourth-grade teacher, though she taught in Aurora Public Schools from 1949 to 1970. In her brown suits, sheer blouses over mysterious layers of lingerie, still reddish hair, and stern but affectionate demeanor, she inspired a blend of loyalty and terror. Mrs. Frandsen made me the goat with blistering criticism when, hav-ing been dispatched to the shopping center with a small committee to buy supplies for a room party, I failed to wait for the crossing guard when we re-turned. But when I jammed a sharp pencil, just like this one, into my palm as I fumbled and tried to catch it, she walked me over to Dr. Rowan's office herself.

For a few of us who cared, she was also an intense source of pride, for Mrs. Frandsen was the author and illustrator of *Our Colorado*—the official fourth-grade social studies text adopted all over the state. The blue-bound book told the history, geography, and natural features of the state through a narrative involving a Colorado family. A published novelette she called *High in the Rockies,* long before John Denver, told the further adventures of her characters Joe and Alice. Her simple drawings of lark bunting, blue spruce, Colorado blue columbine, maps, and miners en-livened the slim orange book. She'd inscribed my copy "Dear Bob: May you always enjoy reading about Colorado." After our reunion, she sent me her late sister's copy of *Our Colorado,* with its plain, clear writing. She loved the language, and her diction would be rare in the classroom today.

Mrs. Frandsen was the first author I had ever known. I was impressed, because books mattered to me. Thornton Burgess's Bedtime Stories, *Life's* *The World Around Us,* A. Hyatt Verrill's richly anecdotal *Shell Collector's Handbook,* Emil E. Liers's *An Otter's Story,* Ernest Seton-Thompson's *Wild Animals I Have Known*—these books were friends of mine, and their authors my idols. So to have an author as my teacher felt very special. A somewhat distracted pupil, I found I did not mind the pedagogy got up as story; it had all the zing of my favorite part of school, being read to from our classroom reader, with the added feature of having some natural history built in.

Mrs. Frandsen cared about nature. She taught us about conservation, and what it meant to her. If she recognized a bud of interest in these topics in a student, as she did in me, it brought an undisguised blush of delight. When we wrote poetry in Mrs. Frandsen's class, she encouraged nature and conservation as subjects. And when we wrote something memorable to her, she kept it—asking us to copy our poem into a blank black book, and to illustrate it with crayons. She entitled the book *Treasures: A Collection of Poems Written and Illustrated by My Pupils in Grades 4 & 5.*

On this visit to Mrs. Frandsen forty years later, she was ninety-five. We had lemonade with her daughter Dorothy Goddard on Maude's warm summer porch. Maude referred to me as "the little boy of long ago," and recalled episodes that I had long forgotten. Halfway through our visit, she brought out a Brown & Haley chocolate box. There within the tissue innards lay a black book—*the* black book—replete with the fourth-grade poems of Leslie Coxsey, John Culley, Rae Dichter, Bobby Pyle, et al. We read several of them together, remembering my classmates, her students. When it came time to leave, Mrs. Frandsen said she was eager to have me back when it was cool enough for coffee in the kitchen, her Swedish idea of proper hospitality. But the following winter she died. And a few months later, I received a package in the post. Opening it, I found the candy box, the black book, and the poem.

In the Forest

In the forest lives the deer,
Brave, bold, and sincere.
In the forest lives the porcupine,
On his back, his shiny spines.
In the forest lives the bear,
He looks like a hunk of hair.
In the forest lives the skunk,
With a stripe on his back like a little chipmunk.
In the forest lives the raccoon,
Washing his food by the light of the moon.

—Bobby Pyle (1956–57)

I'm no longer sure about the brave and bold part, except so far as both are synonyms for survival; or sincere, except as all wild animals are infinitely sincere, knowing nothing else. On reexamination, my poem offers little promise of a literary career; nor had I yet given up the common practice of calling all animals "he." But the point was, when asked to write, I wrote this. It may be the first nature writing I ever attempted.

Not that it was the only impulse. Once when I was in second grade, my big sister and I found ourselves with a big book of wallpaper samples, blank on one side. Susan (who wrote Western stories with a female hero named Sunset Ames) and I decided to write a book called *Seal Rock* on the sample book, probably inspired by Walt Disney's True Life Adventure *Beaver Valley*. She would write the text and I would help and draw the pictures. (I'd spent long Saturdays at the old Aurora Public Library copying pictures of seals, otters, and sea otters in Crayola, wearing out my brown crayon.) This epic came to naught, but in third grade I did type out lists of seashells with their scientific names on one of my grandmother's typewriters, cribbing from her *Britannica*.

My grandmother, Grace Phelps Miller, was a scholar and a gardener in whose book-filled home and prolific East Denver garden I roved widely. But it was her daughter, my mother, Helen Lee Lemmon, who first drew me into the natural world. I remember her walking me home from kindergarten and pausing to investigate the life of a rotting corner stump. And from her own garden, as she weeded the violets and irises, she plucked cocoons and other intriguing live things to show me. I'm not sure why my initial fascination for natural history settled on seashells, but they consumed much of my attention from ages seven to eleven. By fifth grade, I noticed there were more butterflies around (many) than mollusks (none) and switched allegiances.

The first book I purchased in a bookstore with my own money was Alexander B. Klots's *A Field Guide to the Butterflies of North America, East of the Great Plains* (in the Peterson series). My other sacred texts were W. J. Holland's *The Butterfly Book* and, especially, my treasured copy of *Colorado Butterflies* by F. Martin Brown. Inspired by Brown's monograph, I began keeping a field notebook of my butterfly observations and formed big plans for writing scientific papers describing the new species I tried to discern in minor variations of common butterflies.

If Mrs. Frandsen got me excited about the Colorado peaks, it was F. Martin Brown who actually drew me to the high ridges. In *Colorado Butterflies,* he wrote about a black butterfly called the Magdalena alpine:

> This large and uniformly black Alpine is a real prize. It can not be confused with any other Colorado butterfly. . . .
>
> The Magdalena Alpine haunts the rock slides at timber line. . . . Once in a while conditions have been such that a large brood of the species is produced. Then if a collector is around he has a field day.

I loved the brown butterflies known as satyrs, such as the chocolate, eye-spotted wood nymphs I found along the banks of my nearby habitat, the High Line Canal. But there was something about this all-black relative, with its intriguing name, and the other arctic-alpine butterflies, that beguiled me completely. Whenever I was able to get into the Rockies, clearly visible from our Aurora subdivision but untouchable across the intervening city miles, I aimed for the tundra and the high rockslides beyond. Such a field trip would end in one of the fundamental meetings of my life as a naturalist.

In the late fifties and early sixties, I spent a week or two each summer at my stepfamily's cabin in Crested Butte, in the West Elk Mountains on Colorado's Western Slope. "Crested" was a paradise of fritillaries and swallowtails, sagebrush and aspen, habitats and butterflies I had only imagined from the pages of Brown's book. To escape the endless smoky bridge games in the cabin's kitchen, my father and I fled to the nearby trout streams. While he cast with dry flies, I plunked with a spinner until I grew impatient with prey I couldn't even see, and ran off with my butterfly net into the adjacent meadows. Through boggy pastures perfumed with red and white clover, I pursued silver-bordered fritillaries and gilded Sonora skippers.

On one such outing during the summer of 1959, I rambled up to a ridge overlooking the meanders of the East River, below the old silver-mining ghost town of Gothic. Cresting the shoulder, I looked down in astonishment to see a flailing flock of people with butterfly nets. They were the only other collectors I'd ever encountered in the wild. I was an excruciatingly shy child, but I overcame my embarrassment to go down and ask who they were, and what was going on.

The netters turned out to be students from the nearby Rocky Mountain Biological Laboratory (RMBL), with their professor, Charles Lee Remington of Yale University. I recognized the name immediately. Remington was the cofounder of the Lepidopterists' Society, which I had joined earlier that year. Standing next to the tall, young, ginger-bearded prof, I knew I was in the presence of one of the country's foremost butterfly scientists and became tongue-tied. When he asked what I was interested in, I got out, *"Sir-SIGH-oh-nis."* "Oh, *Cer-cy-O-nis,"* he replied. At least he had understood my poor Latin for the wood nymphs. And from that encounter grew a remarkable association.

It turned out that Paul Ehrlich of Stanford, another well-known butterfly investigator, also came to RMBL for his summer research. For several summers after that, I hung around with Doctors Remington and Ehrlich, often hunkering in the corners of their cabins drinking Cokes and listening to the erudite butterfly talk that passed around the room among these living gods and their graduate acolytes. Ehrlich and Remington not only tolerated but encouraged me, occasionally even driving me up or down the serpentine eight-mile cart track between Gothic and Crested Butte. And during the third summer, the annual meeting of the Lepidopterists' Society was actually held at Gothic. I met many others I'd read about, and even some collectors my own age. There could have been no greater inspiration to a young naturalist than the ties this random encounter brought about, and they could not have had a greater impact later on.

On my thirteenth birthday in 1960, I hiked to Copper Lake above Gothic, at Remington's suggestion, and first laid eyes and butterfly net on a big black Magdalena alpine, coursing up and floating down the high and wild screes.

Another butterfly trip first took me across the high ridge, to "the opposite slope of artistic imagination." After my mother died in 1967, many papers were lost among her moldering files in my grandmother's leaky garage. But somehow, a manuscript survived that revivifies that event. I had written it in ballpoint ink on the green-runed letterhead of the Millsite Lodge in Silver Plume, Colorado, a few weeks after I graduated from high school and four days after my eighteenth birthday. I was working that summer before college as a private contract lepidopterist, collecting montane butterflies for a dealer in New York City—an experience that paled as the value of living butterflies necessarily shifted from passion and beauty to mercantile units. But it did get me out of the city and into the mountains every day, all summer long. My mother, always my best collecting partner, had accompanied me on a butterfly expedition to the Western Slope. On our way back to Denver, the weather trapped us behind a slide-closed highway.

I had not been encouraged in writing or in biology during high school. I carried my *Origin of Species* around in my back pocket, and I like to think a little of the graceful language seeped in along with Darwin's boundless curiosity. But my assigned biology teacher was much more interested in his other job as football coach, and later abandoned both for dry cleaning. The two teachers who truly enthused over nature, Ed Butterfield and Keith Anderson, rescued me part-time with their Ecology Club. Otherwise, I sought natural history largely on my own, and it was the same with words.

I knew I had a verbal facility from taking the standardized tests, and I could use it to lubricate grades and to win cash and prizes for citizenship "essay" contests. But no one introduced me to personal, lyric prose, and poetry was pretty much confined to "Thanatopsis" and "The Rime of the Ancient Mariner." We were taught mechanics well, if we paid attention, but there was little encouragement toward free expression. As was standard for that generation, when we were taught "essay," what teachers really taught was exposition. No one invited us to assay the world with that sweet blend of observation and opinion the world deserves, and in fact demands. And when I once essayed to write something from the heart, I was accused of plagiarism. My written response to the natural world remained objective field notes from my ditch, which I imagined as my answer to the Galápagos.

Stuck in that flooded canyon with my mother, when I had work waiting back in town, I wandered behind our motel impatiently . . . and ended up scribbling the first prose I can remember writing because I was purely and simply moved to write it. Seized with the desire to get away from everything man-made, I'd scrambled up a rain-sodden slope that was greener and more luxuriant in growth than anything I'd seen all summer. Eventually I slipped and tumbled down and landed in a verdant, mossy situation that made me laugh with the freshness and wildness of it. When I got back indoors, I wrote and wrote on the motel stationery. In part, I recounted:

> Rather than righting my position, I remained on my back in the wet and clean mossy moisture, and watched, and listened. At that precise

moment, a truth (came) to me—a truth so simple that I felt I had always known it but needed only to have it revealed to me dramatically: When one has love in his heart and the greenness of nature about him, no one or no thing can take away from him or despoil for him the very real beauty and wonder of life.

The words were neither original nor profound, but I felt that they were; and the pages they appeared in comprised my first real essay.

That interlude among the uncharacteristic moss of Colorado also proved delphic for the two-way approach I've taken to the land ever since, drawn back and forth between the arctic-alpine heights and the maritime rainforest. I came by my love of the mountains honestly, born into a Colorado family that owned several ranches high in the Rockies until the Depression. My grandmother Grace and her sister Helen prowled the jeep trails and mine roads for decades in a succession of autos from Model As to Volkswagens. But they had also gone to Washington as young women, where they were pioneer teachers in remote locations. My mother was born and spent her girlhood in Seattle. I grew up hearing stories of head-high ferns, cool fresh rains, and deep ravines that were green in midwinter. I believe that I imprinted on the maritime Northwest vicariously, even as I imprinted on both the grasslands and highlands of Colorado in person. So it was not out of character when I wrote, in that summer storm outpouring, that in arid Colorado I had missed much that only the rains can instill and that only those who stay out in the rains away from the fireplace can discover: Everywhere, everything was painted with the green-beseeching brush of wet, wet rain . . . Eventually I heard a rushing rivulet and hurried to see it, lest it all run away before I got there . . . I always welcome a mountain stream (and) wish I were a portion of it, hurrying over the un-complaining stones and through the green-wood which is always greenest near it . . . Even in the dusk, the green remained, and deeped; even the single animal I saw—a moth—was green. I caught him, watched him, and let him go—he was perhaps the most beautiful green.

And it was no fluke when, after my mother took me for a pregraduation look, I chose to leave Colorado behind for college in verdant Washington.

When I followed the rain and moss to my mother's natal city of Seattle, in the fall of 1965, I immersed myself in the moist verdure I'd so thirsted for in Denver. I walked endlessly in the green ravines my mother had known and loved as a girl. And I plunged into conservation activism as a founding member of the University of Washington's Conservation Education and Action Council (CEAC).

I became politicized over Vietnam. (In junior high, I had been appalled by a demonstration of napalm at an air show east of town. Now I saw what it was for, in photographs mounted in the student union. I made a connection very fast, nudged along by a Greek Row parade with a banner that read "Kill a Cong for Christ.") I applied my newly awakened activist ardor to fighting for the North Cascades National Park, against dams in the Grand Canyon, and on behalf of habitats on our own burgeoning campus and around a Seattle that was about to blow out into the hinterland.

At the same time, I abandoned the prescribed curriculum for zoology majors. Having anticipated deep immersion in nature in and out of the classroom, I found the lab-oriented, quantitative science requirements oppressive. I flunked chemistry twice in favor of ardent birdwatching, and I pursued instead a self-styled program in natural history and conservation, taking great advantage of the survivors of a passing generation of faculty naturalists. With their encouragement and assistance, the studies I wanted fell into place.

And I wrote. At the outset of 1967 I began keeping a journal, pretentiously titled *Chronicles of a Naturalist,* which I have maintained in various forms and intervals of entry ever since. By this time, I was reading John Muir and aped his language of praise for the glorious wild, self-consciously but not well. My own thoughts and perceptions did seep in, however, and it wasn't long before I shed the mock Victorian naturalist's diction and began to explore my own means of expression. My journal was, at first, largely a vessel for the celebration and description of field trips. I felt moved to record the many new organisms, landscapes, and fields of knowledge I was exposing myself to. It was also a record of places, people, and events, and a sounding board for constant academic trauma and uncertainty about what might follow. The journals grew increasingly personal and descriptive, a preview of the high-grade ore they would one day furnish for my books.

From that year on, I also found means to publish my writing. One of the first pieces I wrote for publication was an obituary for my mother, who died during my second autumn away from Denver. She was well loved among the butterfly folk who knew her. The piece appeared in the *Journal of the Lepidopterists' Society*. That was followed by a number of butterfly notes and papers in that and other journals, intended to make available my observations (which I saw as being in the grand tradition of descriptive natural history) and early thoughts on Lepidoptera conservation. For less specialized pieces, I exploited campus magazines, newspapers and Sunday sections, and the newsletters of local conservation organizations, which were always crying for copy.

The most important early venue for me was the *Northwest Conifer,* the magazine of the Puget Sound Branch of the Sierra Club. In return for helping to staple copies, the editor let me publish accounts of wilderness beach backpacks, or whatever else I wanted. Sparked by my first conservation classes, readings, and a summer abroad, I wrote issue pieces and enquiries with ponderous titles such as "On Immensity and Usufruct: European and American Conservation, a Comparison," "Four-Wheel Drive and the Outdoor Experience," and "Conservation and Natural History."

On rereading these early essays, I note how close

my concerns then were to my present feelings. In "Conservation and Natural History," I wrote about an experience in a downtown pocket handkerchief of green that I frequented, Denny Park. I'd been thrilled to see a hermit thrush among foraging fox sparrows on the lawn. "Just then, a group of tiny children entered the park from one side. They paraded through, kept in rigid file on the pavement by teachers in front and behind. A little boy stooped to pick up a splendid maple leaf, and raised it toward his teacher with an excited, 'Look!' Blank-faced, the teacher took the leaf and herded the child along without reply. I thought, can that child's nature wonder survive, or will it vanish like the summer green of the maple leaf? And when he is grown, will he care if a forest is saved?"

That essay was a bald statement of personal philosophy, much influenced by Joseph Wood Krutch's neovitalistic writings. At the time, no doubt partly inclined by my disastrous dances with physical chemistry, I was unwilling to entertain the likelihood of a mechanistic world, which I saw as inimical to conservation. These feelings would evolve, and so would those about the land and its users. My attitude came from exposure to certain teachers, devoted activists, and readings, and from my own involvement in land-use campaigns—including a distant effort to save my beloved High Line Canal. Every time I went back I found Denver's suburbs greater and greater, the habitats of home lesser and lesser. These changes hurt my heart, but also imbued me with an element I would never again be able to rid from my writing, even if I'd wanted to: call it a conservation conscience.

My early campaigner's voice sometimes came out sounding sanctimonious, strident, and absolute, traits that the radical never abandons altogether. I distrusted compromise then (after all, there *is* no compromise with a dam, or an open-pit copper mine), and I'm still not the keenest fan of an elusive "balance" that commonly translates into still greater loss of already depleted treasures. It shouldn't be surprising that much of my writing in those days was righteous rhetoric in service to conservation.

Mine was not a literary college education. The only two writing classes I had after my freshman year were both excellent: "The Short Story," from Jack Cady, who had parlayed a truck driver's seat, publishing in *Overdrive* magazine, into a college teaching position via the *Atlantic Monthly* "First" Award; and "The Magazine Article" from Linda Daniel, an accomplished journalist. Although I had published a number of essays and articles by then, I got a comeuppance in the article class, because I wrote tendentious polemics on conservation themes, full of personal opinions and aesthetic description, rather than objective articles.

In Cady's terrific class, though his inherent kindness let me down easy, I wrote an execrable short story that was really a preachy morals tale arranged around an oil spill. I would spend afternoons in the original Red Robin Tavern, in a torn vinyl booth, sipping thirty-five-cent glasses of elderberry wine, listening to Bob Dylan sing "The Gates of Eden" on the jukebox, looking out at the gray rain on Lake Union's houseboats, and scribbling drafts of my story, which was

31

also called "The Gates of Eden." But the course had an impact beyond what I managed to write. I remember Cady coming to class one night and having difficulty staying dry eyed. Every few minutes he would tear up. Finally he told us the reason: John Steinbeck had died that day, and he was having a hard time coming to terms with the loss. I had never seen anyone so affected by a writer, and his emotion made a deep impression. It caused me to read Steinbeck more thoughtfully than I had in high school, and I was thrilled by the way he compounded story and the nature of the land. In his fine new book *The American Writer,* Cady shows that his feelings haven't changed: "When the fires of the twentieth century are banked, the one writer who may continue to stride through history will be John Steinbeck."

Needless to say, no one offered a class in the lyric essay at the University of Washington in the 1960s. But haltingly, I discovered what it was on my own, while learning the value of accuracy and subtlety in my conservation rhetoric. All along, thanks to butterfly study, I knew how to observe and record detail closely, and these habits were honed by great teachers such as ornithologist/mammalogist Frank Richardson and mycologist Daniel Stuntz. Ultimately, natural history came together with politics when a band of us took over the university wetland in the fall of 1969. While others occupied the administation building, we occupied the Montlake Fill, a wondrous marsh leased to the city of Seattle as a dump.

I had canoed the marsh frequently, birding and avoiding chemistry classes, and regarded it as a lucky relic of former times. Later, I was horrified to learn what had been lost when I read Harry Higman and Earl Larrison's *Union Bay: The Life of a City Marsh.* The two consummate naturalists described, in 1951, an ecosystem that still worked fully in the shadow of the city, where otters, beavers, muskrats, weasels, and mink all bred. What we knew fifteen years later was a mere shred of the marsh that had been. And the bulk of it had become a noxious landfill, stinking and barren, where only gulls and rats were happy.

On that autumn afternoon, several hundred students, faculty, and other conservation activists marched from the Husky Union Building to the Montlake Fill in a classic sixties action dubbed the "Union Bay Life-after-Death Resurrection Park Plant-In," or, for short, the Life Park. Having demanded topsoil and trees and gotten them, we planted firs and pines all over the fill. Professors Frank Richardson and Art Kruckeberg brought plants from their own gardens and spaded them in, working alongside their own inspired students. Our trees would all die eventually in the methane-infused mire, but that day led (through decades of meetings and drudgery) to one of today's great inner-urban habitats. As the leader of the action, I was asked to write up the event for the Sierra Club's 1970 mass-market paperback, *Ecotactics.* The essay "Union Bay: A Life-After-Death Plant-In" marked my first time between the covers of a book.

That exercise led to an assignment for *Audubon* to write about Willapa Bay, the great estuary near which I live today, threatened by many factors even then. From these two pieces, I began to learn how natural history fact, personal aesthetic, and conservation responsibility might be blended in a form that respected fact, art, and ethic without sounding like a tract. *Union Bay* probably showed me this more than any other book at the time because of its direct relevance. Earl Larrison brought the accuracy of the old-time observing naturalist; Harry Higman lent the book more of its heart, and together they managed to wed them well, through a bond of the love they shared for a magic place and the deep concern they felt for its fate.

I was also reading Rachel Carson, Aldo Leopold, and William O. Douglas, as well as Margaret Murie and Victor B. Scheffer, both of whom I actually knew. I wanted to believe that I could write books like theirs. Mardy Murie was the widow of the highly respected wildlife ecologist Olaus Murie, and an activist in the Wilderness Society. She was a fine writer in her own right, and her books *Two in the Far North* and *Wapiti Wilderness* were college favorites for many of my friends. I rode side-by-side with her on a bus journey to Burns, Oregon, to testify before Senator Mark Hatfield's Minam Wilderness hearing—fourteen hours of piñon jays and inspiration. Mardy and Olaus had been instrumental in the passage of the Wilderness Act of 1964, and she has continued as special advisor to the Wilderness Society ever since. Residing in Moose, Wyoming, in the summers and in Seattle in the winters, she made a point of encouraging young conservationists whenever she could. Trips to her cabin on San Juan Island to investigate the equally colorful tide pools and spring wildflowers, and to see our first orcas, deepened the dedication to conservation that JoAnne, my wife at the time, and I already felt.

In the spring of 1970, when I cobbled together my early essays to submit for a Dutton environmental book competition, I asked Vic Scheffer to write a fore-word. Like Olaus Murie, he was another long-time government wildlife biologist and a superb natural history writer, the author of *Year of the Whale* and *Year of the Seal*. Vic had performed the sea otter research and writing that I had dreamed about as a boy. About my book, he wisely suggested we wait and see if it would actually be forthcoming. The thoughtful editor at Dutton, while encouraging, recommended that I seek more of a common theme than my unripe ef-fort, humbly dubbed *Nature Matrix,* actually pos-sessed. But Vic's supportive friendship and example, as he continued to create a stream of intelligent and memorable books, gave me much more than I had asked for.

A meeting with Supreme Court Justice William O. Douglas added one more huge measure of inspira-tion. In the spring of 1969, CEAC invited him to hike with us to oppose Kennecott Copper's plans for an open-pit copper mine in the North Cascades, some-thing Douglas had done to resist roads along the wild Olympic coast. To our astonishment, he ac-cepted. During the event, a well-publicized hike up the Suiattle River, JoAnne and I lunched with Justice Douglas and his wife Kathy. We were awestruck, but I noticed his deep attention to the natural history around him. My mother was a devotee of his

Washington books, such as *My Wilderness*. And when JoAnne and I later read his revolutionary *Wilderness Bill of Rights*, I remembered his craggy face on that forest hike, the set of his jaw, and knew exactly where that radical ethic came from.

I finally graduated, but only with the assistance of a sympathetic dean, who helped me hammer my courses into a general studies degree I called "Nature Perception and Protection." Dean Aldon Bell required a senior thesis, a long, never-published lyrical essay entitled "A Mineral King Aesthetic," based on a summer's rangering in Sequoia National Park. And he asked me to take one more quarter of classes that drew my themes together around communications. Through one of these, "Principles of Nature Interpretation," in the College of Forest Resources, I met my first postgraduate mentor. Professor Grant W. Sharpe, after distinguished service with the National Park Service as a ranger-naturalist, had become the recognized leader in the field of nature interpretation, and ran a graduate program of interpretive studies in his School of Outdoor Recreation. I found a ready home there, and worked as a teaching assistant for Grant while taking a master of science. My thesis became my first book: *Watching Washington Butterflies*. I battled my committee over how much, if any, lyric sensibility and personalia I could slip into the pages, and increased it substantially between thesis and book form. The book was published by Seattle Audubon Society due to the enthusiasm of Hazel Wolf, the society's secretary almost forever, now recently deceased at nearly

102. Hazel, and her late housemate Emily Haig, were important teachers of mine, too; Emily had belonged to the Sierra Club when John Muir was still president! I felt that, through these remarkable women, I had a direct link to John O' Mountains himself.

Before leaving the University of Washington, I taught writing for the first time in a class of my own concoction called "Nature Communications." With Grant Sharpe's assistance, I took a succession of interpretive jobs in parks and other agencies, but in stages came to recognize that while the work was good and important, it wasn't for me. The intellectual and artistic limitations of interpretive writing, and rangering's necessary degree of repetition (never a long suit of mine), overcame the conservation potential of such work. I left interpretation to pursue conservation science, but I took with me Sharpe's refined sense of simple, elegant use of the language on nature's behalf. His classes may not have been concerned directly with "creative writing," but the concepts he drove home have everything to do with my hopes as a writer. In addition, his attention to the effective use of slides and speaking has helped subsidize my writing life ever since.

As the campus Fulbright advisor in 1970, Sharpe alerted me to the program. My application to study butterfly conservation in Great Britain must have touched the fancy of the selection committee in those ecoconscious times. The fact that I had established a relationship and earned an invitation to study with John Heath, zoologist of the British Biological Records Centre (BRC), no doubt helped. A

Fulbright-Hays Scholarship delivered me up directly to the Monks Wood Experimental Station in Abbots Ripton, Huntingdonshire, west of Cambridge. John Heath became my next great mentor. With him I learned how to characterize the landscape in terms of its butterflies, and vice versa, through the practice of applied biogeography. By mapping the natural distribution of British butterflies, then comparing ebbs and expansions against conditions on the ground, the scientists of the BRC created a powerful tool for plotting conservation needs. Their colleagues at Monks Wood were conducting the ecological research to undergird species management programs, based on these map-driven priorities, and I studied with them as well. My Monks Wood apprenticeship furnished the focus for whatever science I have undertaken since, as well as one of the finest years any naturalist could want.

John Heath himself, who died too soon in 1987, was a graceful writer and widely published entomologist who brought me back to the precision of scientific observation and description that I had slighted by shunning hard science as an undergraduate. But I also formed a profound and lasting attachment to the English countryside and to the nature writing it has inspired, from White, Jefferies, Hudson, and Hardy on.

On and on over the hills I ranged, in search of the rare heath fritillary. Not named for John Heath, but his favorite butterfly just the same, *Melitaea athalia* had dropped out of most of its former range in

England, according to the BRC's maps. My applied project was to try to catch a clue as to why. Accordingly, I spent much of the summer of 1972 revisiting former heath fritillary sites to try to characterize how they differed from still-prime habitats. Of course, I took the chance to explore all the other butterfly sites I could in the charmed countryside of pre-Common Market, pre-Thatcher Britain. Much of what I saw, largely unchanged since medieval times, would be altered or lost in the next twenty years. At the time, I remember thinking how little was left, and treasured the remains perhaps less than I might have. Even so, it was a charmed season.

In the Lake District, I pursued one of the Magdalena alpine's two British relatives, the mountain ringlet, on high Helvellyn. The other one, the Scotch argus, actually flew out of the heather practically into the kilts of a busking bagpiper I'd stopped to watch on the Pass of Glencoe in the Scottish Highlands. I went out with Jack Dempster, the ecologist studying the survival of the British swallowtail in the last wild corners of the mostly drained fenlands of East Anglia. I accompanied another ecologist, Mike Morris, on a nocturnal expedition into the sucking darkness of Borth Bog, on the Welsh coast, in search of the endangered creature known as the rosy marsh moth.

But my field work centered on southwest England. After helping John Heath teach a butterfly and moth course at Nettlecombe Court Field Studies Centre in Somerset, I rambled the nearby heaths and downs of Exmoor. There I encountered, among purpling heather on sandy patches in the sun, the grayling butterfly of Tinbergen's famous experiment in courtship behavior. I climbed Brean Down above Weston-super-Mare, where blinding white chalk soils nurtured calcicolous legumes whose flower buds fed the larvae of uncommon butterflies. Chalkhill Blues, pale flecks off the Bristol Channel, flittered over the particolored down turf in their hundreds. And with Jeremy Thomas, a fellow Monks Wood graduate student who would become Britain's foremost butterfly conservationist, I scaled steep combes on the Cornish coast to see the very last habitats of the vanishing large blue butterfly, an extraordinarily specialized ant symbiont on its way to extinction for then unknown reasons. Naturally, we retreated to many a country pub to process our findings.

On the lip of a lush green ravine in deepest Devon, reminiscent of my Seattle haunts; and again on one of Prince Charles, the Duke of Cornwall's estates tucked into remote Cornish countryside, I found colonies of heath fritillaries still healthy in extent and numbers. These I contrasted to several sites on Dartmoor and elsewhere, in which I found rank vegetation overwhelming the fritillaries' (Americans would say checkerspots') plantains and related hostplants. In one such site, I nearly came to grief.

A very old dot on John's map showed an erstwhile colony of heath fritillaries on the daunting slopes of Windcutter Hill near the Vale of Mortehoe, not far above the coastal village of Ilfracombe. Trying to penetrate the place, I was challenged by a shocking array of armed plants. Not only good old British brambles, but also hawthorn, blackthorn, nettle, thistle, rose, holly, iron-spiked gorse, and a number of other botanical booby traps lay in successive wait for the interloping lepidopterist. When I finally forced my way in, using my net to beat back the briers, it was at great expense—and only to find the heart of the habitat converted to Sitka spruce plantation. Not only was this a throwback to the habitat of home, the last tree I expected to find displacing a British butterfly; but it was also one of the stickeriest impediments I'd faced in the entire ordeal. By the time I worked my way out, I was a bloody mess. I threw myself into a shallow bay to let the salt first sting, then soothe my many cuts and welts. In an essay eventually written about the experience, "The Bramble Patch Trap," I wrote that I felt closer to total collapse in that fold of gentle Devon than I have in quicksand, or flailing in deep water close to drowning.

Most of the English experience was more pleasant, and my field work eventually contributed in a small way to what has been a dramatic recovery for the heath fritillary. Directed by Martin Warren, the work was aimed at restoring conditions brought about by traditional forms of agriculture with which the butterflies had coadapted. In a review paper on "Butterfly Conservation Management" that I much later coauthored with Jeremy Thomas and others, we wrote that such land use changes have caused almost all British butterfly losses. Jeremy, acting on that knowledge and his careful research on the large blue, its ants, and their needs, has been able to bring back that butterfly, too, from actual extinction—by getting the habitat back in shape, then reintroducing the Swedish subspecies. Being present at the early days of these developments in butterfly conservation dramatically affected everything that would come later for me.

During my Fulbright year, I was not at all sure what I would do with what I was learning. On the night of December 9, 1971, I attended a talk by British Museum of Natural History lepidopterist Grahame Howarth, at the Linnaean Society, on the future of the large blue. If we lose it, he said, *Maculinea arion* should become a symbol, so that no more British butterflies should ever be lost. On the train back to Huntingdon that night, it occurred to me that we Americans had already lost a butterfly—the Xerces blue, a casualty of San Francisco's expansion in the 1940s—and that the Xerces might well serve as a symbol for our own home-grown butterfly conservation effort.

And so I founded the Xerces Society. Eventually, the group became an international organization for conservation of invertebrates and their habitats. Now based in Portland, Oregon, the society has a professional staff, and a membership of forty-five hundred. Xerces publishes the magazine *Wings* and has been involved in tropical biodiversity, habitat protection and management, aquatic insects, Madagascan fauna, butterfly farming, pollination, and many other issues. The Xerces Society has enjoyed distinguished presidents, including E. O. Wilson, Steven Kellert, and Thomas Eisner. Though I now serve only as an advisor, Xerces occupied much of my political and writing energy over several years, and brought me back together with my first and final scientific mentor, Professor Charles Lee Remington.

I'd known Remington since that chance encounter at Gothic in 1959, and we had remained in contact, if only occasionally. In 1972, he was president of the Lepidopterists' Society, which he had cofounded in 1947. When he received my postcard announcing the Xerces Society, he was in the midst of planning the twenty-fifth anniversary meeting of the Lep. Soc. (as it is known by members). The theme was to be "Endangered and Extinct Lepidoptera." He wrote and invited me to take part in the meeting. I took a week out of my English field work, borrowed the air fare, and flew to San Antonio. The occasion became the formal launch of the Xerces Society. Before I left Texas, Remington asked me to come to Yale to continue my studies in a doctoral context.

I went to New Haven in the fall of 1973, on my own. JoAnne's opportunities with the National Park Service took her to Alaska, and our marriage, made when we were nineteen, did not survive the separation. Since my master's degree from Washington had been in forestry, I was able to enter Yale Graduate School through the School of Forestry and Environmental Studies. In reality, I was based jointly there and in the Department of Biology. Remington held appointments in both. While Biology and the Yale Peabody Museum have been his primary academic homes for a career spanning more than fifty years, he continues to teach today in Forestry and Environmental Studies. The first American forestry school, founded by Gifford Pinchot, Yale's had recently broadened its mission and become a suitable springboard for innovative conservation science.

Yale made a perfect base for Xerces; if John Heath had been its midwife, Charles Remington was its godfather for the first few years. I was probably the only graduate student in the department with a secretary, provided by a grant from the World Wildlife Fund, U.S., so that I might carry on Xerces while conducting my postgraduate studies as well. Our first annual meeting was attended and supported by Alexander B. Klots, the author of that first book I had purchased in boyhood, the *Peterson Field Guide*; and by Miriam Rothschild, the great British naturalist and conservationist. My second wife, Sarah Hughes, whom I had met at Monks Wood, and I initiated the Xerces Society Fourth of July Butterfly Counts while we were at Yale. Run today by the North American Butterfly Association, hundreds of these counts now take place around the continent. About the same time I began and edited the journal *Atala,* and wrote extensively for that and other Xerces publications.

Charles Remington affected me profoundly, not only during the three years I was his doctoral student, but ever since. I have never known a more exacting scientist, a more mellifluous practitioner of English and Latin, or a more committed conservationist. The way he has managed to mingle these—and still does, in his seventies—on the national scale with Zero Population Growth and on the local, restoring habitats on the New Haven waterfront—has always given me hope that my own unruly pack of interests might be able to coalesce in some satisfying and useful form. His commitment to teaching is evident in a distinguished cadre of intellectual descendents, who teamed to produce a Remingtonian honorarial issue of the *Journal of the Lepidopterists' Society* in December of 1995. My time at Yale afforded me almost daily encounters with an intelligence and resolve so formidable that I was alternately intimidated, entertained, and thrilled, but ultimately reinforced in my own ambitions beyond what I'd ever imagined.

I think of his willingness to sit and talk over problems both academic and scientific for as long as it took, not only with his graduates, but with undergraduates who hung around for the love of insects and received rich encouragement in return. One of these has since become a MacArthur Fellow. Another, attempting to set his first moth specimen during an evening lab, accidentally pinned it upside down. Instead of upbraiding him, Remington peered over his shoulder and said, "Hmmm, clever . . . I see you've chosen to set this moth to display its ventral features." Routinely, during our tutorials in an office stacked to the battlements of the building with lepidopterological works, his hand would shoot out, mantislike, to successfully snatch an irritating fly, his eyes and attention never diverted from me. Another time he was lecturing on the wasp genus *Vespa* in an entomology class, when a huge yellow jacket veered into the room through the open window. "Yes, just like that one," he said. "Thank you very much." The wasp took one turn around the room and flew out.

Remington's finest classroom performance was in his immensely popular evolution course, when he related the legendary 1860 British Association Huxley-Wilburforce debate from the meeting on the just-published *Origin of Species*. Remington himself had enjoyed a Guggenheim year studying with the great geneticist E. B. Ford in Oxford. Back at Yale, he would dramatize both parts in that historic debate, "Darwin's Bulldog" (Thomas Huxley) versus the Bishop of Oxford, in separate accents, finishing to thunderous hurrahs for Huxley. Later in the term, Remington's prize specimen of the Madagascan orchid *Angraecum sesquipedale* always seemed to bloom just when he got to his lecture about how Darwin had correctly pre-dicted the existence of a hawkmoth with a proboscis long enough to exploit the orchid's eighteen-inch nectar tube and thus pollinate the plant—a moth later named *Xanthopan morgani praedicta.*

My initial thesis project, involving relatives of the Magdalena alpine that fly on the alpine slopes and passes of Colorado, hoped to employ some of Remington's hybridization genetics methods. So it was that I landed back at Gothic, at the Rocky Mountain Biological Laboratory, in the summer of 1974, fifteen years after I had met Remington in the meadow above the East River. Again I went afield with both Remington and Ehrlich, but this time as a graduate student instead of as a curious kid. In the meantime, Ehrlich had written *The Population Bomb* and the two of them had founded Zero Population Growth. They and their students and colleagues had made Gothic one of the most distinguished centers of butterfly research anywhere.

That first research attempt got me back to the high ridges of my childhood and led to the initiation of my novel in perpetual progress, *Magdalena Mountain*. But the logistics of the proposed experiments proved prohibitive. Back at Yale in the fall, I confronted Remington with my belief that I needed a research problem more directly related to conservation. At this point, many advisors would have shown me the door. Besides, I had shorted some curatorial tasks and coursework that Remington had set for me in favor of Xerces work. But instead of resisting, he moved mountains in order to adapt the program to my needs and desires. And while he and my committee insisted on a challenging degree of rigor and breadth, they approved a topic along Monks Wood-like lines: an applied biogeographical study, mapping and analyzing the distribution of Washington butterflies in order to measure and predict gaps in the state's framework of nature reserves, coupled with a review of world Lepidoptera conservation. The work went smoothly, and I finished in the spring of 1976—but only because of Charles Remington's rare flexibility, creative vision, and enthusiastic encouragement.

Ultimately, he believed in what I wanted to do and allowed it to happen.

As a graduate student himself at Harvard in the late forties, Remington had known and collected with Vladimir Nabokov. The novelist, years before he wrote *Lolita*, had curated the butterfly collection in Harvard's Museum of Comparative Zoology, where they were labmates. Remington introduced me to both the scientific and literary work of Nabokov. And Nabokov would eventually influence my outlook, both through his uncanny attention to the detail of the world, and by his reinforcing belief that there must "exist a high ridge where the mountainside of 'scientific' knowledge joins the opposite slope of 'artistic' imagination"—where "the Precision of Poetry and the Excitement of Science" can meet.

While I was at Yale, I had hoped to take the vaunted "Craft of Writing" course from William Zinsser. But this class was offered through Yale College and reserved for undergraduates. Other courses I might have found helpful as a writer were closed to non-literature or nonwriting majors. Yet I did not leave Yale without superb instruction in the literary realm. There was one more mentor off campus . . . *way* off campus.

I had long admired Edwin Way Teale, the most widely read American nature writer and the first to receive a Pulitzer Prize (in 1966, for *Wandering Through Winter*). He had accepted my invitation to serve as an honorary councilor of the Xerces Society, numbering among his books some important insect titles. But actually getting to meet him proved more difficult. Several times he and his beloved wife and gatekeeper, Nellie, politely put me off. I respected his desire to reserve his time for writing and now do still more. His delightful book, *A Naturalist Buys an Old Farm,* had made him too easy to find, and many a pilgrim arrived on his doorstep with a book to sign. But I persisted in my requests; and once he realized my serious intention to learn from him, he bid me come. Arranging public transportation to deepest northeastern Connecticut proved almost as challenging as eliciting the go-ahead, but Sally and I managed. What followed were three day-long sessions I can best describe as tutorials on the nature writing life.

Teale was a fit wall of a man with white hair and a steady, surprised smile. Genial but private, he received us, when he finally did, with a full heart and presence. He made us a big salad, then walked us about the premises. He showed us the pond he had made, the gazebo on its shore where he and Nellie had read many books aloud, and the brush pile study in which he lurked to watch what went on around him. Back in his indoor study, Teale told me how he had purposefully prepared himself for a career as a nature writer, including a self-prescribed course of reading that went well beyond traditional natural history. He showed me a teeming yet beautifully arranged array of manuscripts, journals, and ringbinders of memorabilia upon which his books were built—including a list of 451 alternative titles for *Wandering Through Winter.*

It wasn't that Teale instructed me in technique;

we barely discussed it. His books themselves, especially the American Seasons series, and *Springtime in Britain, A Walk Through the Year,* and *A Conscious Stillness*—written with Ann Zwinger, whose own *Beyond the Aspen Grove* had made an enormous impression on me as an elegant literary portrait of a beloved place—provided in their reading a master class on concision, precision, warmth, and simplicity of approach. Nor was it direct advice I came for, though he did give me some: "A book's title should conjure a clear image in the reader's mind," and "Don't go freelance until your career justifies it," which I would flagrantly disregard some years later. It was more his example that mattered greatly to me.

First, that one could *choose* a nature writer's life, and with single-mindedness, preparation, diligence, and talent, pursue it. Second, that the small and the local mattered as much as the dramatic and exotic; he had once leased the insect rights to a Long Island orchard. And third, that it was *all right* for a committed naturalist to pay his conservation dues largely through his writing. Teale lent his name to causes he believed in (like Xerces), but rarely campaigned, sat on committees, or attended meetings. Yet for generations, he brought more people to a loving concern for nature than any other writer in America, doing as much in his gentle, unpreaching way for conservation as the David Browers and Paul Ehrlichs have accomplished through vociferous activism.

The last time I saw Ed Teale was on my way back from a big conservation meeting in the Turkmen

Soviet Socialist Republic, on October 9, 1978. We walked the trails of Trail Wood, beside old stone walls, beneath an October sky blazoned with the outrageous reds and golds of sugar maples. He wore a black-and-white plaid wool jacket that often appeared on his book jackets. Our conversation ran from what he still hoped to accomplish in what would prove to be all too little time, to who were the next generation of nature writers. He said Annie Dillard, his fellow Pulitzer Laureate, had come to see him. He felt she was seeking a kind of blessing. He encouraged her warmly, though he said he couldn't read her more metaphysical stuff.

Teale asked about the butterfly conservation initiatives I was trying to press at the meeting in Ashkhabad, the field trip in the Kara-Kum Desert, and about my writing. I told him that I was already beginning to comprehend that to participate fully in all the arenas I cared most about—biology, nature conservation, and literature, in a world increasingly at risk of loss and daily more engaging—would take several of me. Choices would have to be made. He told me that if I really cared about writing, as he had, that the course would become clear. Ed Teale showed me with enormous generosity what some of the choices could be, as had Grant Sharpe, John Heath, and Charles Remington. Now it was up to me to decide my own mix, and where writing would fit in.

When we left Yale in 1976, Sally returned to England to work for Miriam Rothschild, setting up a museum to attract anglers to conservation at her East Midlands family estate. I would join her, but first I spent the summer in Colorado. I attended a Denver Audubon Society Grassland Institute as a graduation gift from Sally and my father. The bus driver, Mary Jane Foley, also a gifted botanist, suggested that I visit the National Wildlife Federation's Conservation Summit the following week at Estes Park. From this family natural history camp came an invitation that would result in my teaching butterfly and writing classes at some twenty-five NWF Summits around the country in later years. And after the Estes Summit, driving south to Boulder on the Peak to Peak Highway, I discovered what was clearly the proper setting for the novel I had begun a couple of springs before.

The eastern neighbor of Long's Peak in Rocky Mountain National Park, it was a truly mountainlike mountain. It rose in three sharp ridges to a double summit. The knees of the ridges ran down into the pines, but everything above was stone—massive granite outcrops and vast rockslides rising thousands of feet into the azure mountain air. A sign by the highway read "Mount Meeker: 13,911 feet." An old lodge stood across the road, its logs weathered almost black beneath a green asphalt roof, without a garish sign in sight. I checked in and climbed the rustic wooden staircase, its gnarled bannister polished smooth by hundreds of human hands. After taking my gear up to my piney room, I settled into a white wicker rocker on the balcony to watch the mountain as the late sun brought it alive. The western sky contained the summit and the sun, and nothing else.

Each ridge tooth, furrow, chute, and suture stood out, every stone. Out of the olive pink smear grew the face of a mountain whose pocks, wrinkles, warts, and fine features displayed themselves sharply, without reticence. I remained until the mountain swallowed the sun, and I knew I would come back again and again.

Later that July I backpacked in the Sangre de Cristo Mountains with two naturalists from the NWF camp, Mary Jane Foley and Boulder biology teacher Janet Chu. They would become lifelong friends and butterfly count colleagues. Roaming the white cirques of the Sangres, I found Magdalenas among Colorado blue columbines, and felt as if my boyhood mentors, F. Martin Brown and Maude Frandsen, were there with me. It was a last chance to roam the high country of home before crossing the Atlantic again.

We were back in England so that Sally could pursue her own graduate studies in Leicester. I taught conservation and writing courses in a small school with a wonderful name: the Vale of Catmose Village College. Living in a rough limestone cottage in the tiny county of Rutland, among hedgerows, large baronial woodlands full of bluebells in the spring, and still unspoiled countryside, I recovered from the velocity of the three-year doctorate by walking and writing. I filled the voluntary role of chairman of the Lepidoptera Specialist Group of the International Union for Conservation of Nature and Natural Resources (IUCN). This committee was part of the Species Survival Commission, which was chaired by

Sir Peter Scott, founder of the Wildfowl Trust and the World Wildlife Fund, and by far the best known and loved naturalist, bird artist, and conservationist in Britain. He had been knighted for his service in these areas. Working with this kind and brilliant man—and watching him conduct complicated meetings with his gavel hand while painting and writing in his journals with the other—was both an enormous pleasure and a powerful hint that a viable balance might be possible between creativity and activism.

The IUCN work also involved many contacts abroad, one of which led to a job that was both a challenge and a dream for any lepidopterist. When Sally finished her studies, we both went to work as consulting biologists for the wildlife division of the government of Papua New Guinea. She was the botanist and I the entomologist for an appraisal of a plan to conserve giant birdwing butterflies while aiding village economies through a program of butterfly farming and habitat protection. We spent the autumn of 1977 on the island of New Guinea, traveling extensively with government support among the islands, highlands, and coastal rainforests of that most thrilling of biological wonderlands. Almost every day we were immersed among plants, animals, and human cultures of such stunning exoticism to our experience that the stimulus was almost continual. I kept waiting for fatigue to set in, but it never did. Even with a demanding job to do on a tight schedule in a land where there are 740 languages and no word for "schedule," I had so much sheer fun of the naturalist's sort that the experience may never be matched. If it weren't for the infinite richness I find almost everywhere, New Guinea could be a sentence to permanent anticlimax ever after.

Our guide was a tea planter and lepidopterist named Angus Hutton, who knew the country so well that he explored barefoot up remote and wild canyons, and could speak with virtually anyone in the country by some amalgam of pidgin and the languages he knew. Since every day was stuffed with adventure, it is difficult to pull out one more memorable than the rest: would it be the day we walked beneath remnant rainforest giants on the Papuan coastal plain near Popondetta, and a female Queen Alexandra's birdwing—at a foot in wingspan the world's largest butterfly—sailed overhead in defiance both of gravity and all sense of probability? Or the day we met up with Sir Peter in the Trobriand Islands, walked among eclectus parrots, sulphur-crested cockatoos, and Mylar-blue Ulysses swallowtails, and watched the local people play cricket on the beach in full battle regalia? Climbing Mount Wilhelm among wild red rhododendrons and tree ferns to one of the few true tundras in the southern tropics? The geyser basin on New Britain, where big-footed birds (megapodes) incubate their eggs in volcanic soils? Or at Wau, where Raggiana birds of paradise, lekking in their own fiery orange male regalia, competed for attention with flying foxes (giant fruit bats), tree kangaroos, beetles that carry their own camouflage (and ecosystems) of fungus and moss, and the astonishing neon swallowtail called the purple mountain emperor?

Of the people, too, I found it hard to pick favorites: I think of David Pohai, a paramedic who showed us the haunts of the rare Manus green snail on Margaret Mead's island; the Reverend Amen, who rediscovered the Mioko birdwing; highland headhunters turned Jehovah's Witnesses and butterfly farmers; a young couple in grass skirts, grinning and courting over their caterpillar vines on the magical island of Misima; and Blu Rairi, once banned for trading in protected species, then rehabilitated as the consummate birdwing farmer on the Sepik coast.

This day stands out. We were traveling in a dugout canoe toward a small island in the Louisiade Archipelago. Angus knew that a brilliant species known as the celestial birdwing once occurred here but had apparently become extinct. The story held that a party of German commercial collectors had descended on the island years before and collected so intensively that the population had not recovered. (Since they are insects, butterflies are seldom subject to overcollecting; but birdwings, owing to their slow reproduction and the high price on their heads, can be the exception.) The residents of the island had been hostile to white interlopers ever since, especially those with nets, since they had held the celestial birdwing in very special regard and were deeply injured by its loss.

Angus had found the butterfly on a neighboring island, and, in secret, had attempted a reintroduction the previous season. He wanted to see if it had taken, and to reestablish friendly contact with the people.

As we approached the shore, no one could be seen. The entire village had vanished into the bush. We knew we were watched, and that a quick getaway might become necessary. As we beached, I could feel every eye (and potential arrow) boring into my back. Sally may have been the first white woman in shorts ever on that little isle.

Finally, one old man, accompanied by a small boy, came out of the forest. Angus greeted him respectfully, then spoke quietly with him for some time. At last the rest of the people began drifting out from the palms. Angus convinced the village Big Man that a party should accompany us across the island to see if the butterflies were back. It was a hell of a risk. The place had been considered *tambu* ever since the extinction. But the Big Man agreed. Trailing half the village behind us, the children laughing throughout the unexpected outing, we trekked over the island's backbone. The footpath was overgrown, and ran through fields of bizarre pitcher plants. And when we arrived in the far valley, there they were— *Ornithoptera poseidon caelestis,* the vast black-and-white females, the iridescent turquoise males— soaring all about us! Our relief was only exceeded by the thrill of seeing them and the villagers' delight. Later, back in the village, there were tears, happy laughter, and fresh coconuts cut and passed all around.

In Papua New Guinea we helped establish a program that would return income from endemic insects, sold through the Insect Farming and Trading Agency, to the villages instead of to expatriate profiteers as always in the past—income that would relieve pressure on (or even enhance) wild populations and would furnish a rationale for conserving the rainforest near the villages instead of selling it for oil palm plantations. We were asked to extend our contract. But I was eager to get back to the Northwest and to put my experiences to work in a job on home ground.

A forestry classmate from Yale, Spencer Beebe, was running the Northwest Office of The Nature Conservancy. He hired me fresh from New Guinea as Northwest Land Steward, responsible for managing nature reserves and evaluating natural communities in eight states. My demesne included a remarkable array of habitats and management challenges, from restoring Hemingway's beloved Silver Creek in Idaho to reclaiming Hawaiian rainforest overrun by exotic pigs, cattle, and alien passion vines. My favorite preserve in the estate was Cascade Head, whose flowered dome looms over the Sitka Center for Art and Ecology where I would one day come to write.

But there was little writing going on then: the job was far too large for one person. When the Conservancy finally decided to hire individual state land stewards in 1979, I had my choice of states. Instead, at Peter Scott's behest, I returned to England again. There I helped to establish the Conservation Monitoring Centre in Cambridge, and initiated the first *Invertebrate Red Data Book,* for IUCN and the World Wildlife Fund. This volume was a detailed sampling of endangered small-scale wildlife from around the world, intended as a well-documented introduction to the impacts we were making on the animals that comprise most of life on earth. The book enabled innovation of a new category in the IUCN registry of wildlife in peril: "threatened phenomenon," which Lincoln Brower and I had convergently conceived of and applied to the North American migratory monarchs wintering both in Mexico and California. By now I was cochairing the Monarch Project of the Xerces Society with Brower, the great monarch researcher at the University of Florida, and making trips to Mexico with him and others to try to negotiate protective measures for the monarch forests.

While I was still working for the Conservancy, Sally and I had, by fluke, found and acquired Swede Park, an old farmhouse on a tributary of the Lower Columbia River in southwest Washington. When I went to work for IUCN, we began commuting between Gray's River and Cambridge, spending half a year in each place. I was writing the *Audubon Society Field Guide to North American Butterflies* at this end and the *Invertebrate Red Data Book* at the other.

During the years with The Nature Conservancy and IUCN, I did some science, some conservation, and a little writing. What I always came back to was the writing—the more heart-filled, the better. In the end, I think I always knew the words would win out.

"Quickly, look outside!" Thea whispered. I opened my eyes to new snow covering Sitka, and to big brown forms against the white. The nearest wapiti, a cow, saw my movement by the window and froze.

Soon they began moving again—twenty Roosevelt elk drifting through the little campus, beneath our loft window. There was one spike bull and one obvious yearling; the rest were cows, males who'd dropped their antlers and not yet sprouted new velvety tines, or two-year-olds. Massive but compact, their buff butts—I mean color, not condition—bright against their brown bulk, they pussyfooted past. On the way through, they nibbled at apple bark, holly leaves, and Sitka spruce twigs—not the soft new growth that will come in April, but the steel-pin needles that penetrate light gloves. No wonder they pay little attention to the fences in our home valley. To an animal that munches holly and spruce needles, barbed wire must mean nothing.

After the elk moved through, I climbed down the ladder and spent the half hour after breakfast bewitched by the diamonds, emeralds, sapphires, and rubies spangling the spruces. The sun came out, backlighting from the east the dripping boughs. A steady curtain of leaden pellets dropped from melting snow, while a fine dust like last year's pollen filtered through the foreground. In between, pendant waterdrops caught the beams and refracted them like lasers. How a particular droplet shone emerald for minute after minute while those around it were clear; then over here a red, there a blue, another flashing the entire spectrum in cardinal direction rays, arrested me. One great thing about nature writers: we are easily amused.

In 1982, the time came when I was obliged to make decisions. Through both professional and voluntary work, I had arrived in responsible positions in international conservation. I had already declined to devote myself full-time to the Xerces Society, to accept a long-term research and advisory post in Papua New Guinea, to continue in stewardship at The Nature Conservancy, and to manage the species monitoring unit in Cambridge. But through my work with the Species Survival Commission, I was poised to advance in the IUCN hierarchy in Switzerland or elsewhere. Any one of these situations would have provided a fine platform for a contributory career in biological conservation and policy, and they were all tempting in their own ways. Besides, the IUCN connection had already taken me to far-flung and exciting locations, such as the national parks of Kenya and Costa Rica, where, as a naturalist, I reveled.

But that was the problem. I noted again and again how my colleagues, friends, and acquaintances in similar jobs tended to become severed from the source of the impulse that had brought them there. People who began as naturalists, biologists, or at least nature lovers, who were moved to work in conservation out of the ideal to protect what they loved, with few exceptions became office and airplane bound, prisoners of committees, meeting-mired. They seldom went out-of-doors with any depth of penetration, and ultimately lost their motivation in favor of other rewards: salary, security, and power. Sir Peter was a striking anomaly who still spent every possible moment out-of-doors. But he was an artist and a naturalist first, outside the professional realm. Others who maintained field devotion either had independent means, a supportive university appointment, or were almost pathologically busy to the exclusion of any private life. Serenity did not often figure in.

I feared such a metamorphosis in myself. Further, I was put off by the illusory self-importance I saw among the international conservation establishment, and by the bureaucracy, factionalism, pointless paper production, and accommodation with hostile forces that permeated much of the profession. I could not abide, for example, the fact that the chief executive of World Wildlife Fund-International at the time was on loan from a South African tobacco company; nor could I live with IUCN's motto morphing from "conservation with development" to "conservation *for* development." I was glad that some people had an appetite or at least a tolerance for this climate, because I had no doubt that the essential goals of these groups were right, and they managed to accomplish much important work. It's not that I came to consider professional conservation as either misguided or corrupt. But it was a branch of the Big Muddy, and I was ankle-deep in it. I chose to leap for the tangled bank of the shore and hang on. Institutions need team players, and I'd abandoned Little League, football, and wrestling in favor of solitary discus-throwing and my old ditch. For all it implies, I recognized in myself a much stronger impulse toward the individual effort: whenever possible, out-of-doors.

The other career path I had strongly considered, even assumed as a certainty for a while, was academia. I knew that from a university seat I could support conservation activities while pursuing my scientific interests in ecogeography as begun at Monks Wood and Yale. I could also teach, which I enjoyed and had already engaged in for years here and there, and perhaps write as well. It was the "perhaps" that bothered me. From this vantage, I can see a number of academics who have been prolific writers of essay or conservation rhetoric while producing admired papers and books in their own science, often combining the two most effectively—Edward O. Wilson, Stephen J. Gould, Lynn Margulis, Paul Ehrlich, Chet Raymo, and Bernd Heinrich, for example. But most professors I have known, desire notwithstanding, have written little beyond the mandated papers, letters of reference, evaluations, and committee reports. Though I was quite keen on the idea of a professorial post, I wasn't at all sure it would serve my own goals in acceptable measure.

Besides, the question was, so to speak, academic. Though I read the job announcements in *Science* religiously, and applied widely for a few years, issues of location, timing, competition, or my own traits and needs always militated against a given post. The tight academic marketplace produced several close calls and ugly false hopes that arise in a buyer's market, and ultimately made the decision for me. As I began to age out of the prime hiring profile, I stopped applying for college jobs. In coming years I would take up college teaching on an independent, guest faculty basis. But in the meantime, it took a disaster to force my ultimate career decision.

During the third extended spell in Cambridge, a

house fire befell our housesitters back home. Their lives and the structure were mercifully saved. But the workings of flame, smoke, and water were prodigious and baleful. The place was a hell of a mess. My study looked like something out of the La Brea tar pits. I had fallen behind on the schedule for the Red Book anyway, so I left my job and project in England in the capable hands of my co-compilers, Sue Wells and Marc Collins, and flew back to try to clean up after the fire.

This was depressing work, lightened only by a sunny February and by the fact that my journals and files and library, while smoke-stained and smelly, had not burnt. My dear, long-time cat, Bilak Bokis, had survived too. A few months later, after making essential repairs and scouring, I found myself living with Bokis with no job, money, electricity, water, or telephone—just me, the cat, and the kerosene. My ten-year marriage with Sally was ending, lovingly but sadly. I tried to maintain my conservation roles, but the long trips to meetings I was used to making became impossible. My funding sources evaporated. After missing gatherings in New Delhi, Christchurch, the Soviet Far East, and, finally, an all-expense-paid speaking tour of the Scandinavian countries if I could just get myself to a meeting in Rotterdam first, I lost my momentum and confidence.

Instead of Rotterdam, I went to the hills of home. I spent that wet, dark winter, with its flashes of brilliance in the estuarine sky, roaming the Willapa Hills on logging roads and deer trails, with a can or two of

Rainier Ale and my journal. In the evening I would sit before the woodstove out in the studio with Bokis, write what I'd seen and thought by oil lantern, and read moldy old copies of *The Good Earth* and *Lost Horizon*.

Out of this time came three good things, not that I attribute them to the fire; I'd like to think they would have come in their own good time. But that bleak season, as dispiriting as it was, did serve as a kind of cold refiner's fire to push things along.

First, I decided purposefully to resign several roles of influence in conservation, in favor of an active career choice to write full time, whatever that meant. This flew in the face of Ed Teale's advice, since I had no reserve, nor secure prospects, and earned a small fraction of a decent wage in royalties, and even that was temporary. Some people were upset with me, feeling I'd jumped ship, and others said I was nuts for giving up my "power levers" in international conservation. I was sorry to see the projects I cared about pass on to others who might not care as much, and to lose the excuse for travel to far-flung places. The almost absolute absence of income this decision would mean was a concern. But once the deal was done, I had no misgivings.

Second, I emerged from the solitary period into the partnership of the rest of my life, with my old friend Thea from University of Washington days, who had also ended up single. Thea invited me to come to Wenatchee to see Thompson's clover, a rare endemic wildflower that we had long wanted to visit.

That field trip was the start of our romance. A year later Thea joined me at Swede Park. She brought resources from her previous life that enabled me to keep and maintain the house, and for a temporary but critical period allowed me to experience the truth of John Gardner's dictum, from *On Becoming a Novelist,* that "the best way a writer can find to keep himself going is to live off his (or her) spouse." With Thea came Tom and Dory, my two stepchildren, with whom a close relationship has grown and become especially important to me.

And the third good thing: out of those rambles in the ravaged but moss-bandaged land of Willapa would come *Wintergreen,* the book that defined my trajectory as a writer. But first came another book, and before that, a letter such as every writer dreams of receiving.

The letter came about this way. When I was studying with Charles Remington at Yale in 1976, he sent me in his stead to speak at an American Association for the Advancement of Science panel in Boston on "Wildlife in the Year 2001." My talk outlined an idea I had been developing that I called "the extinction of experience," which says that the loss of common species and features in our own vicinities can lead to a cycle of alienation from nature and consequent further losses. This talk caught the fancy of Paul Trachtman, then-editor of *Horticulture* magazine, and he asked me to submit it. I countered with a proposal for four essays, in return for an advance that I needed to buy an old Volkswagen bus. Remarkably, Trachtman agreed. I got the bus, which was rusty and slow but got me and my stuff from New Haven to my father's house in Colorado (and to Magdalena Mountain). He got the four essays, including the English bramble patch ordeal, a piece on wildlife and the military, another on urban wildlife, and "The Extinction of Experience," and published them in a series.

The *Horticulture* pieces were seen by Roger Swain, well known now for "Victory Garden" on television and for his books, and then a consulting science editor for Scribner. Swain brought my essays to the attention of Peter Givler at Charles Scribner's Sons. And on a spring day, I received his letter: "Do you have any books you would like to write for Scribner?"

Of course I took him up, but I did not go straight to the book I most wanted to write. My track record was for butterfly books, and that's what Scribner bit for—the *Handbook for Butterfly Watchers,* the first national book promoting the watcher's approach to butterflies. I did not, and still do not, oppose sensible butterfly collecting; it can still provide many values. But I did feel that butterflies were seriously neglected as an appreciative resource, and that the more people who care to notice them, the more who will care about conserving them. In the years it has been in print, I've received many letters testifying that the book has indeed helped bring butterflies into people's lives.

The *Handbook* also served as a stealth approach for getting myself between book covers as a lyric essayist. I proposed it in such a way that I was free to write a very personal, often narrative book in the form of related chapters that are really essays. While the book conveys plenty of factual information, the scientific facts are laid out in the context of the author's own adventures among butterflies, in hopes of provoking others to go among them with open eyes. When it came time to propose a second book for Scribner, I no longer had to attempt the difficult transition from reportorial nonfiction to creative nonfiction. The *Handbook* created that bridge between my field guides and what would follow—a series of books in which I could explore what I found when I went forth, and what I believed about it.

Wintergreen: Rambles in a Ravaged Land gave me the rationale and the vessel for a personal, perceptual entrée to the woods, the human and other-species culture of the woods, and the conservation politics of the woods. While it is essay, the very seat of opinion and refracted impression, where a waterdrop may become a ruby in the morning sun and the hills rise in the rapture of orogeny, it is also a factual document of record, where acreage, board feet, and details of events had better be right. What determines the proper relationship of objective and subjective elements of essay, the art and the journalism of nonfiction, is context. The Scribner legal team held up *Wintergreen* for months, to make sure my facts—critical of certain timber companies' upper management—were supportable. I was asked, in the end, to change only one word, which they found charged—"venom" for aerial herbicide sprays. This was not a problem.

I deeply believed that in witnessing to both the subtle but resilient beauties and the enormities of overlogging in this hammered landscape, I was giving free rein to my scientific *and* poetic impulses. The book's reception suggested it was possible to honor both and still be published. Subsequent attempts, however, would not be with Scribner. Another disaster, on a smaller scale than the fire, made sure of that.

In the spring of 1987 I traveled to the American Museum of Natural History to receive the John Burroughs Medal for *Wintergreen,* an award that astonished me and served as the signal event in building my confidence that my decision to go freelance might have been warranted. Around about the time *Wintergreen* was published, Scribner was acquired by Macmillan. My editor, Ruth Singleton, was sacked along with many others, and no one from the company came to the awards luncheon, a remarkable lapse. I was, however, wined and dined in the Macmillan building, as the editor *du jour* spoke with somewhat muted enthusiasm about further books we might do together.

I knew enough to ask to have a chance to bid on the hardbacks when they were remaindered, as most books eventually are, and was told that I could. But less than a year after the award, I learned from my agent that Scribner had not remaindered *Wintergreen.* Presumably to avoid inventory tax and warehousing costs, they had *shredded* it. In my anger and frustration, I chipped two teeth in my sleep—2000 hardbacks of this beautiful book out on the garbage barge! When I returned to New York, no one at

Macmillan wanted to see me. And when my agent and I finally gained entry and an audience with a middle manager, and I asked how this could happen in a distinguished publishing house with any reverence for books whatever, she replied that there still were a few people like that around, but they were not allowed near the decision-making loops. When I pressed for some remedy for the harm done, the manager offered to reprint—at my cost. Charles Scribner's Sons (retained as an imprint of Macmillan), publisher of Hemingway and Fitzgerald and Wolfe, were offering to be my vanity publisher! This experience was better to have earlier, rather than later, in one's writing career.

Happily, the book came to the attention of Harry Foster at Houghton Mifflin Company. With Roger Tory Peterson, Sally and I had already created a butterfly coloring book for Harry. He acquired the paperback rights to *Wintergreen,* and brought it out with the subtitle *Listening to the Land's Heart* (from a commendation by John Hay) to appeal to a broader readership. I have worked with Harry and Houghton ever since. Houghton Mifflin is definitely a business, but one where reverence for books may still be found; it was the original publisher of nature writers from Thoreau to Carson. This incident cemented a deep commitment to independent publishers and booksellers.

Once I had resolved that writing was to be my primary activity, I spent little time pondering what to write, and for whom. Once, interviewing John McPhee for a Seattle audience following a reading of his, I avoided the cliché of asking how he decides *what* to write about—since he seems to write about everything, eventually—by asking how he decides what *not* to write about. He replied that whatever he feels most passionate or curious about is what he addresses when the time to begin a new book comes around. The author Jonathan Raban was asked, after a reading at Elliott Bay Book Company in Seattle, whom he imagines to be his audience. "I don't believe in audiences," he said. "I write for the intelligent reader." Both of these answers seem right to me. I've always felt that I've wanted to write only about that which devoutly interests me, and that if I did it well, I ought to be able to cause lovers of the world and of good writing to care about it. *Wintergreen* and the book that followed it, *The Thunder Tree,* were easy early choices—portraits, respectively, of the land that I inhabit now, and the land that made me. They share a common theme, that of the love of damaged lands, and how best to regard them, other than merely elegiacally: how to love and honor what's left.

In addition, each book introduced ideas that I now consider cornerstones in my building of beliefs. *Wintergreen* is set in the Willapa Hills, a modest rainforest range that was cut over heavily before I arrived in the late 1970s, in some places twice. The book is about being a naturalist in a land of logging and lots of rain. Two other elements I have found here in plenty are mollusks and spiders. As a boy in Colorado, I lived in terror of spiders, and sustained an immoderate lust for seashells, a passion that went largely unrequited in that landlocked state. Eventually I discovered that butterflies were more rewarding, and switched affections; but pursuing them brought me literally face to face with spiders. When I moved to Washington, I found myself surrounded by mollusks at last, and by more spiders than ever. A key essay in *Wintergreen*, "Slug Love and Spider Hate," explores the not-so-very-different natures of obsession and phobia, while plumbing the natural history of the creatures that were the objects of both for me. From a giant Roman snail mating with my finger to a giant New Guinea spider bestowed on me as a snack by a grinnning child, I examine my responses to these animals that aroused passionate feelings for which they were not responsible. (One of the highlights of my literary life was when the slug-sex portion of the piece was read on a late-night erotica program on the radio, along with a story of Nabokov's.) Ultimately, I conclude that the desired state of mind is an elusive equanimity toward all nature.

Especially in the essays "The Sack of the Woods," "The Last of the Old Growth," and "Stump Watcher," *Wintergreen* also measures the endurance of the land and its beauty and fascination in the face of hard handling by humans. Living in a landscape of clearcuts, I went forth to spend time afoot in the absent forest as well as in the old growth. When I tried to approach a timber company about the possible futures of a stand of mature trees across the valley from my home, they responded by quickly cutting the trees in question. That double-cross, my callowness in fingering the forest and the managers' perfidy in betraying my candor, served as a hard rite of passage for my citizenship in Willapa. While sympathetic of the working people who depend upon the forest for their livelihoods, these essays seek the true sources of culpability for laying it waste, locate them in corporate greed and ignorance, and propose where the powers to heal may lie. There is sin in the greenwood, and there can be redemption.

The Thunder Tree gives voice to the principle I call "The Extinction of Experience," first propounded and named in one of those essays I wrote years before for *Horticulture*. Again, its premise involves a cycle of disaffection and loss that begins with the extinction of hitherto common species, events, and flavors of sensation in our own immediate surrounds; this loss leads to ignorance of variety and nuance, thence to alienation, apathy, an absence of caring, and ultimately to further extinction, a dismal round. I came to this knowledge through sad experience. As a young collector roaming the semiwild precincts of the High Line Canal, I found habitats far from aboriginal but which nonetheless gave abundant green relief from the grid of our raw suburban streets. I could range into a patch of weedy mustards and net lovely, uncommon butterflies known by the entrancing name Olympia marblewing. Their down white wings bore apple green bands beneath, flushed with the color of the petals of the wild rose, and indeed their scientific name is *Euchloe olympia rosa*. Eventually I documented the presence of one-tenth of the butterflies of North America along my ditch, from the mountains out onto the plains. But the butterflies, and the habitats, began to drop out dramatically with the rampant expansion of Denver's suburbs. Eventually my own junior high was built atop the Olympia marblewing's haunt, and I never found another site for it near Aurora. After I'd watched enough such local extinctions, and saw how the canal was losing its amplitude for childhood discovery, even as it was becoming used increasingly for recreation, I developed the theory of the extinction of experience. "What is the extinction of the condor," the essay asks, "to a child who has never known a wren?"

The Thunder Tree tells the story of the High Line Canal, as a particular place and as a stand-in for the secondhand lands where most of us gained our sense of the natural world. It is a paean to vacant lots—my favorite oxymoron, for what is less vacant to a curious kid than a vacant lot? The opening essay tells of the devastating hailstorm in 1954 in which my brother Tom saved my life and his own by dragging me into the great hollow cottonwood of the title, while cattle were battered to death in the adjacent field. The great open territory of outdoor initiation is the landscape of the book, and the sanctity of the humble, hand-me-down habitats where our first contact with nature often occurs. But it also insists on personal and collective responsibility for the negligence of natural limits to growth, in this case water. One result of unbridled and unplanned human expansion is certainly the extinction of experience.

When it finally came together, *The Thunder Tree* surprised me in many elements of its construction, which essay should certainly do: if there is no surprise, there is no essay. For example, I knew that the book would tell the stories of the importance of butterflies in my early life, and that it would account for the lives and deaths of my parents. But I had no idea that these would become the same chapters. I believe Terry Tempest Williams's *Refuge* gave me the courage to write this as I did; but when "A Grand Surprise" ended up being about my mother, and "Butterflies in Winter" about my father, I knew that they had come from no place accessible to logic or attribution.

Getting these places and convictions down on paper in a porphyry of my own perceptions imbedded with stories has helped me to question what else I might believe.

One morning at Sitka the elk were bunched up on the meadow below the campus. Thirty of them, all at rest, belly-to-grass with their legs drawn up beneath them, in the sun. Three-toned big deer—wapiti are considered conspecific with Eurasian red deer—sienna heads and shoulders, rich tan torsos, and those buffy butts. A magnificent sight, all would agree, especially so soon after the close of elk season in this Coast Range country of hunters.

Up above the herd rose Cascade Head itself, the one-time ranch that bestowed the meadows, whose leavings became a modest and understated development, the arts center, elk and Oregon silverspot habitat, and, thankfully, The Nature Conservancy preserve. The headland, its grassy plains and rocky point known as the Penacle, loomed white gold in winter weeds and snow. And below the elk, off the estuary of the Salmon River, hammered the high foam waves of winter seas that recently grounded the tanker *New Carissa* down the coast from here.

The head, the spitting surf, the sea—these would be rightly (if blandly) called magnificent. The torn tanker spilling oil off the Coos Bay coast is properly labeled terrible. In the language of Victorian novelists and luminist painters, "terrible" and "magnificent" were often used for the same scenes: appalling prospects that might equally inspire terror, apprehension, awe, and reverence. We have somewhat restricted the definition of "terrible" in modern usage, as we have for "awful." Meanwhile, we have devalued "magnificent" almost to the level of "awesome" by applying it to almost anything greater than "ordinary"—a term which itself ought to be venerated but has come rather to be despised.

The massed elk, the snowy head, the surf may lift the spirits, move the mind, or at least elicit a healthy "wow." They are out of most people's daily experience and, therefore, extraordinary. But what about the far more modest thing I saw when I walked, for a breath and a stretch, down the lane again past the pythonoid vine maples, past the unfurling yellow spathes and spadixes of the skunk cabbage, to the manmade waterfall and the pool behind it, on Crowley Creek? There I stood, assisting cones and twigs on their way to the sea over the several runnels and fish ladders and weirs, when I saw a small brown form flutter near.

The birds along the lane were mostly winter wrens, but they were just tisking, their songs not yet begun, and acting coy. This object fluttered, didn't pellet past wrenlike. Nor was it one of the big brown silk moths, ceanothus or Polyphemus, that would fly here in June. When it came back, there was no question that it was a bat, flitting between drifts of hail and snow at midday. I shouldn't be so surprised at a February daytime bat, having recently submitted a column called "The Element of Surprise" in which another daylight winter bat figured, just the previous month on a warm January afternoon. But this small brown bat wasn't hawking the early midges that emerged in the interval between storms. Three times it mothed out of the alders, swooped before me, and *drank* from the water's surface.

Why not? Why shouldn't a hibernating or winter-roosting bat come out on a mild day to feed, since the nights are too cold, and why wouldn't it be thirsty? But the point is this: I know that big cervids bunch and lie up in lowland clearings in western Oregon, and I know that monster waves crack the coast every day. I even know that gargantuan vessels stuffed with Cretaceous carbons ply the oceans, sometimes breaking and grievously fouling them. But I never knew that small bats come forth to drink by day in bleak midwinter. This may be as good a way as any to back into the hazened country of belief.

When we think we know something, we say we believe in it. Believing something, we feel that we know it. Therefore, when we come to question our deepest beliefs, perhaps we should ask what it is that we really know. Anyone's honest answer is bound to be, "Very little, relative to that which is to be known." And yet, we try to believe in so much.

As it happens, my two latest books have been much concerned with the nature of belief, and how we go about both questioning and establishing what we believe in. Both books also contain mysteries, around which the quest for belief (not necessarily mine) is gyred. Each as well involves a trek, on which my own sense of belief was tested, altered, and expanded.

Where Bigfoot Walks: Crossing the Dark Divide (Houghton Mifflin, 1995) took me afield into the wild Cascades between Mount Rainier and the Columbia River, Mount Adams and Mount St. Helens, for a month. I was not looking for Bigfoot, but looking into it, and into those for whom a belief in Bigfoot is often an article of faith, hope, and cupidity. In *Chasing Monarchs: Migrating with the Butterflies of Passage,* I set out to follow the monarchs' autumn emigration from the West, for two months. Here I intended not only to perceive and characterize a compelling phenomenon, but also to question aggressively a deeply held belief about monarchs that made little sense to me.

In *Chasing Monarchs,* the mystery I hoped to flesh out was how the migration actually proceeds, how the animals live during it, and how they relate to the land while in exodus. The belief I challenged was the received wisdom that claims all monarchs born west of the Rockies winter on the California coast, while all those east of the Continental Divide emigrate to Mexico. But one day in late October 1996, I had trailed monarchs all the way to Douglas, Arizona. I locked my keys in the car that day, it was raining, and I was detained by the Border Patrol as I tried to leave town. But when I finally made it afield, I found the desert broom bushes dripping with hundreds of butterflies as the sun came out. And when some flying past proved to be monarchs, southing strongly toward the nearby border, a moldy old shibboleth collapsed.

The fact that some of the western-bred monarchs also fly into Mexico becomes important when we try to characterize and conserve the threatened phenomenon of the monarch's entire North American migration. But I was also interested in how such a widely held belief came to be: in this case, a very canon of American natural history became established through repetition, hearsay, assumption, and a set of specious data based on recoveries of tagged monarchs that had been transferred from California, released in the Northwest, and recovered in California. Such transfers, of course, are logically meaningless for wild monarchs. So one conclusion, inescapably, was this: when something is repeated frequently enough, it becomes as truth for the many.

But at least monarchs exist: this we know and believe. With Bigfoot, the matter is a little different. As I found, there is no shortage of people who know and believe in Bigfoot. Tracks, casts, personal sightings, consistent reports by sensible and sober people, the 1967 Patterson-Gimlin film from Bluff Creek, and some combination of earnest desire and entrepreneurial self-delusion, along with all manner of hoaxing and hopefulness, cause people to accept giant hairy apes as if they were squirrels in a park or a nocturnal bat catching a moth on a summer's evening. Some of their arguments are quite compelling, even against the obvious objections. As perhaps the first nonadvocate biologist and essayist to investigate and write about Bigfoot in depth, I considered all the evidence closely, while feeling no compulsion ultimately to decide. Among the most interesting lines of evidence is the widespread Native American belief in Sasquatch-like creatures as living elements of their local faunas. At the risk of impolite intrusion, and sometimes with the heartful gift of story outright, I delved into and wrote much on this aspect. But since many Indians seem to see, experience, and believe things quite differently from many Anglos, their experience begged circumspection.

Bigfoot also furnishes a powerful metaphor for wildness. If we come to a time when the forests are so tamed that we can no longer even imagine the possible presence of unknown creatures, I argue, then we will have lost something very profound indeed. In the end, my time afoot in the unprotected wilderness known as the Dark Divide gave forth experience—including a set of tracks—that kept my own mind wide open on the subject of the actual existence of unknown hominoid apes in western North

America. This conclusion surprised me and was, I feel, a remarkable outcome. Yet I frustrated talk show hosts and true believers who wanted me to come right out and say I did or didn't believe. And that I am unwilling to do; because I do not know.

Professor Grover Krantz, an anthropologist formerly of Washington State University and one of the few academics who admits to taking the subject seriously, glosses that issue by his definition of belief. Belief is something you adopt to make yourself feel good, like faith, he told me. He *accepts* Bigfoot in the same way he accepts his other subject of research, Java Man, because the evidence, in his view, supports its existence. Though his *Gigantopithecus canadensis,* described on the basis of footprint casts showing dermal ridges, has not been accepted by other scientists, Krantz's argument for separating knowledge from belief has merit. Yet I have not adopted it. If I say I believe something, I want it to be based on my best state of knowledge at the time.

I tried to explain my basis for belief in the closing essay, "Something in the Night": "An open mind neither rejects nor limits itself to the scientific method but considers it among the other tools for palping the universe. It doubts everything and accepts everyone. It is completely skeptical and wholly receptive, seldom wishy-washy but often unsettled. The open mind is not afraid to be made up, then, like a bed, to be thrashed, stripped, and made afresh all over again. . . . What I want is a state of brain aloof from arrogant dismissiveness, free from superstition, and rich in question. That seems to me the only way of approaching Bigfoot that would be acceptable to the subject—and the only way to be a naturalist."

As I was writing this about belief, a reggaelike song came on the radio, performed by a group called Inca Inca. Its refrain went, "No one can say what I believe." Really! Well, maybe no one *can* know. We can try to convey what we think we believe. When the radio further informed me that the effort, to that point, had failed so far to salvage the beached freighter *New Carissa* and the Coast Guard and the Navy were now going to try to burn its oil before coming storms could break it up, I was inclined to accept that the reporters believed these facts themselves, and thus to believe them myself, for the moment. If they later said that no oil escaped, I might have been inclined to reassess their veracity.

I am a conservative on the question of essay versus fiction. Sure, memory is selective and refractive, and the remembered truth may indeed *be* one's truth. But this is different from disingenuously offering up imagined scenarios as if they really happened that way. In *The Thunder Tree*, I wanted to relate the fierce and devastating hailstorm of July 1954 as it actually happened. I trusted my memory for many details, compared it with the memories of my siblings, and researched the microfilms of newspapers to confirm as many facts as I could. I found that the hailstones really were grapefruit-sized, but that no kid was killed by the hail, as I had long thought. If I had then gone on to report that a child had been killed, though I had learned otherwise, it would have been not lyrical refraction, but lying. As I said earlier, I feel it is the essayist's duty to furnish a contextual roadmap for navigating imaginative prose while recognizing and relying upon text with all the field marks of fact. But the willful conflation of fiction and nonfiction, which some seem to advocate rather than honoring their slippery edges, merely licenses breaking faith with the reader.

From an early age, I have felt that what I understood to be faith arises, for me, from nature; and nature (in other words, everything) is far too complex to begin to know. But we can know bits, or bits of bits. Sips, as a small bat might take above a waterfall. These are all I have to work with.

I walked down the grade to the lagoon behind the bar of the Salmon River's outflow, the sun welcome in my eyes. At the waterside I looked for whomever might be around. The obligatory lone heron, head tucked under wing, stood on a sand point. A few herring gulls slipped over my way, then, finding nothing on offer, slipped away again. A disconformity on the smooth surface of the water resolved into the wedge of a harbor seal's head. The seal surfaced and peered twice. The rocky beach was a boneyard of white limestone and a brickyard of red mudstone. I sat on a log and watched a pod of common goldeneyes drift down with the current, dive, rise, struggle to swallow small fish, dive some more, then fly upstream to drift and dive down again. The females' heads were coffee brown when wet, the males' purple and greeny black with the big white spot, and their black-and-white wings etched like an Aleut pattern of fish bones.

Over the bar, moderately gigantic waves slapped seastacks and broke over their tops, or raced toward the beach breaking like a chorus line of spouting whales. The coming storm, which would make still larger combers, ate the sun as it turned the water from silver to pewter to putty. There would be no sunset like the one Thea and I watched after the snowstorm, when the West went blackberry mauve and every cloud had a salmon lining. But for a while the sun shot great godbeams through the leaden curtain, lighting up the wild, wild waves. Then the tide turned, shoving a gentle but persistent wash up along the sand-shore on the lagoon's far side, swooshing, purling, eroding the edge, and lifting the goldeneyes ever so slightly. A pair of bald eagles materialized over Cascade Head. They swung round and round, almost meeting as their spirals intersected, round and round. Finally one of the pair dropped below the horizon. The other continued to rise, high above the Penacle, until a red-tailed hawk flew out of a cloud, dove on it, and pursued it off to the east.

Not every scene has mammoth waves, rugged headlands, and bald eagles, but every setting has just as much to notice, if our powers of perception are keen enough. Yet it is the grander, wilder, lovelier scenes that tend to excite expressions of reverence. One of the first ways I knew my impressions were out of line with the norm was that what most excited reverence in me as a child seemed to do little for others. When my stepmother's family visited the Black Canyon of the Gunnison, I shared their awe at the deep dark gash; but they did not reciprocate my excitement over the patch of white thistles, covered with golden skippers and Queen Charlotte's fritillaries, that we passed on the way. I knew my devotion was not solitary, because when I returned to the Black Canyon with my mother years later, she shared my unusual focus (and many more years later, people eager to pay good money for me to take them to see the Colorado hairstreaks and canyonland satyr butterflies proved there were other nuts like me). Still, it has been true that my sense of the sublime seldom coincided with what were supposed to be the sources of sublimity.

My walk down to the lagoon also reminded me of another mismatch between my temperament and what I have commonly heard from others. Beholding those picture-book sacred sunbeams, those eagles, the power of the seas, the Black Canyon, or the surprising elegance of color and form of a silver-spotted fritillary, people often say: "When you see something like that, you have to believe there's a God who made it." I never felt that it demonstrated any such thing.

Not that my immediate family insisted on such a conclusion. Neither my parents nor grandparents ever lobbied for a deity in the household. There was only the palest of connections with the Methodists, likely just a name to fill in on forms, and a place to wear new Easter clothes. I wore a terrycloth robe as a wise man in a local Lutheran Christmas play, and perhaps attended Sunday school a time or two; but I quit them forever the day the Lutherans paved their parking lot, wiping out the marshy corner that held the only colony of bronze coppers for many miles around.

I remember, in junior high, coming across a reactionary rant in the Sunday *Denver Post* religion section, condemning a tendency toward "syncretism"—an acceptance of a bit of this doctrine, a bit of that—which the author felt would lead to watered-down Christianity, then no doubt to relativism, secular humanism, godlessness, and on straight to hell. I co-opted the word in an earnest attempt to embrace the goodness of all teachings with my pagan leanings. I called my invented religion "naturo-pantheistic syncretism," as my brother Howard still reminds me. And for a while, along with the well-worn good book I carried about in my hip pocket *(The Origin of Species)*, it served to quiet those who would proselytize me. But it wasn't long after taking instruction from a genial and lenient priest to marry my Catholic girlfriend, that we immersed ourselves in the woods and in the writings of naturalists, and both her Romish ways and my ecumenical mish-mash fell away like discarded pupal exuviae.

After my father's death at sixty-six, my sister-in-law Mary—a conservative Christian—and I were talking. We often baited each other and jousted, in a friendly and loving way, about evolution. That day she said, quite seriously, "You know what we Christians really can't abide about evolution? It's that evolution requires the extinction of the individual personality." I realized that she was right.

My early essay on mechanism and vitalism argued for something unknowable in life beyond mechanics. I know now that, as earnest as this was, it grew partly out of my bad attitude toward chemistry; but there was also the promise that vitalism held out for the reunion with loved ones, in some form. I was especially susceptible to such thinking after my mother, my great friend and field companion, died when I was only twenty and she fifty-two. I can't say exactly when the change came, but eventually I accepted that individuals do not transcend death, and grew to take great comfort in the fact that our materials carry on in ferns, waterbears, and rocks. And now I wonder whether our corporate eagerness to behave, as Robinson Jeffers put it in his poem "Calm and Full the Ocean,"

> as if man's world were perfectly
> separate from nature's, private and mad

might not come from our reluctance to relinquish ourselves to the earth along with everything else. Witness the concrete vault and fiberglass coffin that would keep my father's molecules from the soil for centuries. (My mother's ashes and bone bits went to a dozen places she had loved.) I found I believed that "ashes to ashes" means relinquishing our souls (or selves) to the earth as well as our bodies, and that I do not differentiate between the two.

The time came, in my thirties, when I wished that I had paid more attention in chemistry, though I never rued the rabid birding I'd done instead. More to the point than any intellectual objections to a caring god, I came to have no objections to an absence of deity. The mysterious I loved; the mystical, on the other hand, became a fuzzy sort of croker sack for any kind of mystery that people were too self-centered, lazy minded, or unimaginative to ascribe to the infinitely generous workings of an utterly indifferent universe. And this may be putting the case a bit harshly, because after all, what do I know? But so it seems to me.

The English novelist Martin Amis, in *The Information,* says of astrology: "And what was astrology? Astrology was the *consecration* of the homocentric universe. Astrology went further than saying that the stars were all about *us.* Astrology said that the stars were all about *me.*" That argument sums up for me most of the metaphysics with which I am acquainted. The stilling presumption of astrology, that the workings of the cosmos could somehow center in on one's personal and piddling affairs, seemed to have much in common with the assumptions of many religious outlooks: quite natural to hope for, and very likely biologically adaptive under certain stresses, but untrue.

What came to offend me especially about some flavors of resurrection-based religion was the assumption that, since a better world awaits, what happens in and to this one is ultimately insignificant: the apocalyptic cop-out voiced so well by Ronald Reagan and, quite explicitly, by his calamitous secretary of the interior, James Watt. This view of the world has been repudiated by many faiths currently aligned in restoring a sense of responsibility for "the Creation" under the rubric of green theology. Surely this is a good thing, to focus religious fervor toward environmental needs. Still, I think a sharper sense of conservation consciousness might come from faith in the fact that what you see is all you get. I, for one, find great joy in the workings of weird coincidence and comfort in the wackiness of what-it-is.

Beyond the misuse of religion to the detriment of cultures and to the rest of nature, I harbor no hostility toward anyone's experience or expression of religious faith, though I do admit to a certain impatience with the instant oatmeal that passes for ideas among many of the self-described spiritually driven, especially in its "New Age" manifestations. I recognize the good that can come from a religious inclination among individuals and communities. But in the evolution of what I know and believe, I have come to value the physical as if it was all there is, and to conclude that it probably is. Since I do not find the physical wanting, I do not want for the metaphysical. The very concept of the supernatural implies a presumption of essential poverty on the part of the natural, which I find distasteful. Mind and heart, as well, are one, and if you need a place to put the soul, the spleen or the sacroiliac will do.

This, then, I believe: Heaven is here, angels are

butterflies and bats, and the great beyond is the holy compost pile of the ages. It is the same for bollworms, Bigfoot, thee, and me, so we'd best make haste to live well in the here and now, with our eyes and hearts wide open, in kindness and generosity toward our own and other species. That, to me, would seem an ample world in which to believe, and for which devoutly to hope.

The next day at Sitka came dry and cold, the spaces beyond the treehouse windows painted in crisp greens and browns and straw. High winds and rowdy weather were expected again. The first attempt to explode the oil on the *New Carissa* fizzled. I considered resurrecting that short story I wrote in Jack Cady's class some thirty years ago, "The Gates of Eden," to see if there was anything in it for a modern oil spill.

Those offended, disappointed, or hurt by a material view of the universe might fairly ask: So what does it matter, an oil spill, if there is no accountability to a higher power? Why write about it? Why, in fact, write about anything? Or, like the young man I saw buried in a copy of *The Fountainhead* on a New York subway recently, why not just go with Ayn Rand; if the world is a material one, what's to say selfishness isn't just the ticket, and damn the oiled birds and beaches? That question rightly deserves an answer. It is, after all, me doing the asking; the part of me that sentimentally wishes for a world of consequence, reciprocity, and meaning.

In fact, I think that all those things exist, but

only in our minds, which makes them no less valuable. I absolutely honor and covet and celebrate the impulses of sublimity, reverence for the sacred, love sensual and soulful, subduction of the self in poetry, music, ideas, truth, and another person's mind or body, and ardor for particular elements of the world. And I feel that all of these arise in response to chemical and electrical stimuli both from within and without. That my delight, exaltation, awe, and horror all issue from neurons connected through synapses devalues them in no way. But that understanding liberates me from the tyranny of demons and the jealous and fickle favors of gods. When I pray, and I do, I recognize it as an expression of hope for good breaks, and an invocation to myself to act in such a way as to harvest the possibilities of hope from happenstance.

Such a view recognizes the full powers of free will, within the constraints of physics and chance. I have no patience with any flavor of fatalism. If we are free of the tyranny of devils, we also give up their usefulness as scapegoats. This means that one of the wonders of the Indifferent Universe is that our responsibility actually *means* something: we have neither the constraints nor the restraints of fate to fall back on. We *are* ultimately responsible for what happens here in our social overlay on the given world. And this, I believe, is the really significant difference between ourselves and other intelligent animals— only *we* possess the power to affect things on such a grand scale, *and* the tools for decisive restraint. That is not to say that other species never make decisions;

I am sure they do. But the scope of their decisions to alter the world around them is much more limited than ours. We *can* spill oil; we *are* responsible.

When the editors of *The Norton Book of Nature Writing* decided to include a selection from *Wintergreen,* I was surprised at their choice of chapter. Instead of one of the more natural history-laden essays, they picked "And the Coyotes Will Lift a Leg," a bare-naked philosophical piece in which I first attempted to express some of these ideas. I wrote that "my humanism ends where we become so fond of ourselves that we cannot imagine the mortality of mankind," and that my faith lies in "the perpetuation of my matter in crocus, coal, or comet . . . [the knowledge] that atoms continue in nature." But I also put forth my sense of "cosmic optimism" based on a cheerful acceptance of the dictum that "nature bats last." While I take solace in the ultimate freedom of the earth from our abuses and find it much more difficult to sustain a midterm optimism in view of the thoroughness of those abuses, I nonetheless maintain that a rationale for hope and a basis for better behavior actually exist. And herein lodges the sanguinity with which I am temperamentally afflicted or blessed. I wrote:

> Of course, another reason for short-term optimism lies in our ability to apply will and thought and action to effect change in our time. We can create a nature reserve and enjoy it for the rest of our lives. We can vote the bums out. We can live selectively, choosing that which we wish to experience. And there are,

after all, far too many pleasures available to be able to sample them all: too many wild and intriguing places to ever visit, people to meet, birds to watch, symphonies to hear, and so on. The riches embarrass our poor ability to enjoy them. Pessimism in the short-term is its own punishment, since it vitiates the will and makes one a pawn of circumstance.

I could have added, there are too many books to read, and that will always be true, and too many bookstores to visit, though that would have dated the essay, which was composed in 1985. Since then, of course, one of the greatest and most grievous extinction events of our time has occurred—that of the independent bookshops, laid waste by the predatory tactics of the chains. Selection, in the human realm, where there is often nothing natural about it whatever, can be vicious. Natural selection acts to enhance the adaptive vitality and suppleness of creatures and the systems they comprise altogether, whereas corporate "selection" often acts to diminish the diversity and stability of community. When ignoble book barns squash neighborhood bookstores (halving authors' royalties in the process— those deep discounts must be made up somewhere), a suitable and defensible analogy can be made with the loss of species diversity in ecosystems. Corporate aglomeration drives systems toward simplification, whereas local complexity furnishes the suppleness that favors stability. Or simply say that diversity—in species, cultures, publishers, bookshops—makes the world a hell of a lot more interesting, tolerable, joyful, and—let's face it—fun. And fun counts. As Bruce Springsteen put it in "Badlands," "it ain't no sin to be glad you're alive." This, too, I profoundly believe.

How does my view of the universe pertain to the question floating on this cold Pacific air, which is, Why write? Having determined for my own purposes that we are at play in the fields of the come-what-may, believing as I do that both the culture and the species are finite and maybe not so damn far in the future at that, why participate in an act whose very sincerity would seem to depend upon faith in society?

Dr. Johnson said the only reason to write is for money. Well, since I decided that writing would be my chief work, nearly twenty years ago, of course I do write for pay. The income I derive from writing is helpful in buying my independence. I rely more upon book advances than on royalties (which are almost a thing of the past for midlist writers), and on fees for occasional pieces such as reviews, forewords, and articles. But the results would not impress most people in these market-conscious times, and I must augment them as best I can. The vague pay is certainly not what keeps me writing.

The chance to influence others drives much of what I write. Precisely because I feel this is our one time through the world, I think we owe it to ourselves to seize every opportunity to protect, preserve, restore, and defend the very qualities that our economic activities ruin, despoil, or place at risk. And for as long as I've written, I've felt that naturalists who take their pleasure and heart from the land have an inescapable duty to speak up for it—and to convince and encourage others to do the same. We write letters to editors and agencies as well as articles and essays meant to change minds, incite activism, and inspire others to rave and rage on. Specifically, I write for the last old growth in the Willapa Hills, against the proliferation of toxins especially through roadside and forest spraying, for an eventual Dark Divide Wilderness Area in the Gifford Pinchot National Forest, against habitat damage that affects rare butterflies and other invertebrates, for the conservation of migratory monarch butterflies throughout the Americas, and against threats to my own watershed, among other targets.

I also write to share events that have amused me and experiences that have moved me. To record and validate my own experience, both objective findings and subjective impressions, and to experience the particulars of the world is one thing. To preserve them is another. I write to express, unburden, or fulfill my mind and heart, especially in poems. I write to entertain myself, especially with stories. I don't think I write for the notice it brings. On the whole, any notoriety writers come by is extremely relative in a culture that values literature somewhat less than monster trucks and much less than pro wrestling. "Fame," such as it is in our arena, serves chiefly as an impediment to living and a distraction from actually writing (as I well remember from Edwin Teale's experience). While flattering, public attention swipes time out of all proportion to the additional book sales or other satisfactions it is likely to bring. As for immortality, there is none to be had. But I do like the idea of my words outlasting me, popping up years from now in a dusty secondhand bookshop or on a library shelf. This is one reason I prefer putting my words into books over more ephemeral media.

Many writers say they write because they must. Well, I suppose I must. But this tic could be serviced by my journal or by correspondence. That explanation doesn't account for thousands of hours sitting on my rear working hard when I could be walking, birding, butterflying, dancing, making love, reading, sleeping, playing, conversing, or drinking good ale. When I consider all the other reasons I write, I realize that virtually all of them leaf out of love and concern for the world. I find that I cannot strictly separate my artistic or scientific impulses from my conscience in this, and if I try, the results are unconvincing.

Maybe excepting only human population and acute chemical pollution, the greatest threat to a sensible environmental future is nature illiteracy. In earlier cultures, most members of the community were capable naturalists, familiar with many other species around them—or else they perished. There was strong adaptive pressure to know your neighbors. Even in our culture, nature study was considered a standard part of the public school curriculum, and familiarity with local flora and fauna, a basic and durable skill. Nature literacy went out between the wars, and was given a good strong punt out of the park by Sputnik—just when I came along, and found that my interests were considered passé in public school.

Environmental education has never really taken up the slack. Urbanization, the extinction of experience, and the virtual in lieu of the real exacerbate the case. Outdoor activities are extremely popular, but contact with plants and animals runs only skin-deep for many, so that a state of mass detachment from nature prevails.

Without any question, my most important classes in school were typing and plant taxonomy. Botany 113 from the great botanist C. Leo Hitchcock at the University of Washington (Thea, a botany major, took it too, and worked for Hitchy in the herbarium) introduced me to a lingua franca for interpreting the green world—the families, and basic relationships, of plants. Such a knowledge allows one to feel grounded and among friends anywhere. As Ann Zwinger puts it in *The Nearsighted Naturalist*, when she goes to a place with a new flora, it's like "walking into a big party where at least I know a few families and recognize some friends (nice old Mr. Agave, dear Aunt Mustard, and dearest friend, Anemone), people I can talk to with a modicum of familiarity."

What is the importance of nature literacy? Besides allowing one to feel situated, more grounded than the usual state of ignorance permits, it can have the consequence of causing one to care: it is harder to bulldoze friends than strangers. Of course, our widespread lack of intimacy with nature sets up environmental illiteracy, and together they deliver a powerful double whammy to the people caring for the land.

Eventually, I could have taught myself to type,

but it is much harder to learn the basics of life's forms without instruction, whether it comes from a wise uncle of a hunter, a grandma in her garden, or a professor. But wherever we get it, as a people we need to know more about our living surrounds than we do. Botany 113 should be a prerequisite for graduation in any major; should be a required class for life.

I like to think that most of what I do is a blow, or at least a breath, against nature illiteracy, from butterfly field guides to essays to poems to the field courses I teach for summer institutes of natural history. I tell students that a nature writer can be thought of as an amanuensis to the land: the land speaks, we take dictation, and by dint of great attentiveness, care, love, and luck, we might get some of the words right. That applies to my work, I feel, whether attempting to characterize a butterfly in precise scientific terms, or to paint a page-picture of the world with imagination and lyrical whimsy. I fully believe both approaches are necessary for survival.

I write to try to help give biophilia a chance to blossom. The great Costa Rica-based biologist and writer Alexander Skutch put it perfectly: "Those who care greatly because they appreciate greatly have no more sacred obligation than to do everything in their power to preserve the kind of world that will nourish appreciative minds for countless generations. Appreciative, cherishing minds are the world's best hope."

The world as I perceive it is infinitely rich, enthralling, and delightful, and at the same time deeply, appallingly, unutterably sad and flawed. The good bits owe to both natural and cultural riches (if I may so differentiate them for simplicity's sake, knowing that the culture is part of nature). The regrettable aspects are all human imposed, excepting of course the great levelers—disease, natural disaster, and mortality. Many have found existence to be intolerable, whether due to pain, oppression and poverty, loneliness, meaninglessness, fear of death, or various species of depression, madness, guilt, or remorse. I do not count boredom; I have no sympathy for the merely bored.

Considering war, torture, genocide, ecocide, and the full, loony spectrum of brutality and incivility in the world, and the threats they pose to peace, happiness, and survival; imagining the dopey embrace of affluence at the expense of the earth and the blue mantles of the sea and the very sky, anyone would have to be Pollyanna in rose shades and earplugs to feel chipper about the state of things.

But there are balms: neither opiate nor snake oil, nor yet panacea, but a cool and scented cloth to the heated brow; relief, encouragement, temporary amusement, sympathetic succor, even as much as hope. Nature is such a balm, one of the best—intimate contact with a world that works and remains sublimely indifferent to all human harms. Literature is another; it can help make life more tolerable, more worth living. Good nature writing is a nostrum that combines the best of both, one I have often relied upon for my own relief. If I can help a reader to see or feel the world as a richer place, or impart pleasure or a fuller heart through my words and experiences; if I can mitigate a stifled existence or enlarge a full one, that would be reason enough for writing.

The best part for me is the immense satisfaction gained from the intimacy with the world that the work requires. To write about the forest, the valley, and the homestead where I dwell, I have no choice but to burrow in deeply and shuffle about. Who else gets to examine home ground as closely as a shrew, and call it a job? Who gets to go into the Cascadean wilds for a solid month, or up and down the American West for two whole months, in search of truths and lies about butterflies and Bigfoot? Who gets to go back to the charmed territory of childhood to find what's left and what's lost but not forgotten? To know other life forms as one who writes their biographies presumes to know them? And best of all, to plumb the exquisite depths of his own ignorance, and indulge it again and again by tossing new facts, impressions, heresies, whimsies, and dreams into the bottomless well? I get to do all this; and whatever I decide to do next (as long as I can interest my editor in the same thing).

Paraphrasing an old hunter I know, I write because it gets me out. Like going to the compost in the morning, fetching the mail, or peeing outside at night, which I just did. The February night has gone very mild, and I am very spoiled. I just can't imagine, is what it comes down to, doing anything else.

February 12, Charles Darwin's birthday, was the last morning at the Sitka Center in Russ's Treehouse. The woodstove sat cold. It wasn't just balmy outside, it was positively vernal. The last little streaks of snow, held in the lee of the broad-lapped spruces, were sublimating in the light warm west wind. Thea returned from a walk to the lagoon with news of the first magenta salmonberry blossom. Up on the slopes behind the cabin, huge spruce no more than a hundred years old interspersed with elderberries—torso-thick, recumbent, moss-pelted trunks sending up numberless pocked and brittle red elder shoots about to explode in green. The entire, friable hillside was spattered with the heart-shaped, succulent leaves of miner's lettuce. They erupted from elk-hoof hollows, from moss-trapped motes of soil in the elbows of trees, from the turf itself. One day not many weeks away, the entire *Picea-Sambucus* forest would pop with the candy-striped colors of *Montia*'s blooms.

I took my coffee, an old white ceramic Tony the Tiger mug of it, out to the cabin's deck. The bathroom was remodeled before we came, and the old toilet resided temporarily out there. A couple of days before, its porcelain took on a whiter shade of pale beneath an inch of bun-shivering snow. This morning, in the dappled sun, its call was seductive. From its pleasant perch I watched yellow shavings fly off to mix with the shed scales of spruce, their storm-shed cones and needles, and all the good detritus, as I sharpened my twelve pencils for the sixth time. They were much shorter. It was a good morning. The Navy's napalm, they said, had done its job, redeeming for now its old fell purposes, burning off much of the oil of the *New Carissa* before its broken hulk could be towed out to be sunk in the deeps. It was Darwin's birthday. It was, for the moment, though one would be a fool to think for good, spring.

In the forests of the Maritime Northwest, two species of geometrid (earth measurer, or inchworm) moths erupt in the earliest days after winter. *Mesoleuca* is half-white, as its name states, half black and blue and chestnut. *Enchorion* is cocoa brown and cream. Both appeared for the first time that morning. A third moth, whose name I don't know, a close mimic of the rusty spruce bracts lying all around, lay flat against the cabin wall, a fine emblem for Darwin Day.

Charles Darwin became a bright light for me because of a series in *Life* magazine in the fifties, featuring his life and work. I wanted to turn my room in our tract house into a natural history laboratory like his study at Down House in Kent, a shrine I have often visited. I obtained a paperback of *Origin,* carried it around like a charm, and still have it, the most worn of several editions I own. It was the first really challenging book I read, and its precepts informed my earliest drafts of a philosophy, as they have the latest. But it was not until much later that I realized how the final paragraph of the book is one of the most graceful and pungent passages in the language: "It is interesting to contemplate a tangled bank," it begins, "clothed with many plants of many kinds, with birds singing on the bushes, with various insects flitting about, and with worms crawling through the damp earth," and concludes that "whilst this planet has gone cycling on according to the fixed law of gravity, from so simple a beginning endless forms most beautiful and most wonderful have been, and are being evolved." Some say that Darwin was strictly a writer of science, but there is poetry here. And in the absence of genetics, his divination of natural selection as the foundation of biology definitely entailed the imaginative act as well as deduction. I have described how I came to know I could write, and why I do. I've also mentioned the struggle that showed me that the poetic proclivity was probably stronger in me than the scientific, and the ways in which Nabokov and others showed me that I needn't absolutely choose between them. Darwin, too, has always remained a model, as one of the most careful and brainy watchers at the tangled bank there has ever been.

That watching, to me, is the key. I am fortunate to have the platform for a sustained voice in a column, "The Tangled Bank," in *Orion Afield*. In as many forms as I can muster, the message is always a variation on the manifest delight, refreshment, and downright redemption to be found *out there*. I write these essays not just to convince others to step out, though I do hope for that; nor to provide readers with vicarious experience as refracted through my own tinted, scratched, bent, and dented lens, although there is that, too. I confess that I write them also to remind myself to truly *live* the days and nights; and to live them anew in the writing. After all, none of my beliefs mean a fig if I don't drop everything else and betake myself out-of-doors, and frequently. My capacity to share the world with others is only as good as my own experience.

But even Darwin couldn't stretch time. When Wallace came nipping at his heels, he finally had to publish; otherwise, he might have written drafts forever. He *seemed* to find a way around time, writing an astonishing succession of books comprising a virtual library of natural history, beginning with barnacles and the *Beagle,* running through insectivorous plants and orchids, and finishing with worms. But he retired beneath a slab in Westminster Abbey before he got to zooplankton.

Nabokov, too, had to make decisions about how best to use his time. Though he believed, and proved, that one could perform good science while committing serious fiction and poetry, and teaching to boot, doing all three wore him out. After the success of *Lolita,* he felt compelled to subordinate Lepidoptera to literature, returning butterflies to the status of avocation. In *Speak, Memory,* Nabokov wrote, "I confess I do not believe in time. I like to fold my magic carpet, after use, in such a way as to superimpose one part of the pattern upon another. Let visitors trip." But time caught up with him, all the same. Before he died, he lamented that a certain butterfly was emerging, and that he would never see it again. He left a novel and several major butterfly projects unfinished. Edwin Teale, too, passed before completing everything he had to say.

Time *is* the rub. Of all the nature writers I've

read, maybe only Jack Kerouac claimed to have a handle on it. As he had Dean Moriarty say in *On the Road,* definitely a nature book, *"We all know time."* I take this to mean that time, no matter how much or little of it he had, would not get the best of him; he would spend it just right. (Few book reviews have pleased me more than a recent one for *Chasing Monarchs* in the *Cleveland Plain Dealer,* comparing the book to *On the Road,* with the monarch in the role of Dean Moriarty.) Moriarty was based on Neal Cassady, and perhaps he, and Jack, really did know time. But Cassady and Kerouac and Dean Moriarty all died young.

I don't want to die young. Like Springsteen, "I want all the time, all that heaven will allow." And since my conviction is that heaven is to be found in deep attention to the billowing brilliancy and ordinariness of the world as we find it, it seems to me that the way to know time and to honor the world is to use the days as well as can be.

I have never suffered a crisis about what time well spent means for me. I've never regretted a minute spent out-of-doors with my eyes open. Reading a heartfelt novel, story, poem, essay, or letter has never caused me to feel I was injuring eternity, though many Christmas letters, e-mails, newspapers, and magazines are another matter. Dancing is always time well used; so is birdwatching, and listening to the blues in all their various manifestations, from Bach to Brahms to Bartók, Bobby Burns to Bobby Zimmerman to B. B. King. Love, family, friends, and good cats. The night. Walking by day with my butter-fly net. Hiking any trail, exploring small roads that may go nowhere. Conversation and meditation make for moments no more squandered than taking a memorable beer in a satisfying setting, whether it be the Free Press Pub in Cambridge or my old chair sur-rounded by books and warmed by the woodstove at home.

However, I distrust drunkenness, and always, even in the days of the Life-After-Death Resurrection Park Plant-In, rejected drugs beyond a few introduc-tory cannabine snacks. I cherish too much my native perceptions, which I consider to be the very sub-stance of life, to wish to alter them beyond what binoculars can do for me. When the young ask, I tell them that nature is my drug of choice.

I am social, but I require much solitude. I have grown almost anaphylactically allergic to most kinds of meetings, to nearly all committees, to automobile parts stores, and to sports bars. I have not had televi-sion for thirty years, and so am a lost soul in a hotel room with a remote control. The radio is a frequent companion. Oh yes, finding ways to spend time well is easy. But what is not always appreciated by aspi-rants is the sheer quantity of time this occupation takes. The real challenge is to honor the hours neces-sary for getting the writing done, since nothing will stop the time, and nothing will make more of it. I do not expect an ATM ever to ask me, "Do you need more time?" and mean it.

A nocturnal animal by nature, adapted for social purposes to the day, I need a full ration of sleep. At home, I awaken at 8:30 with assistance, then read to morning classics often until the gift of Garrison Keillor's daily poem on the radio at ten. Arisen, I carry the chamber pot to the compost heap to get moving and breathing. I write the rest of the morning, either back in bed with its cheap warmth and inspiring view of the covered bridge and valley, or a few steps away at my desk, or at a table on the front porch on fine days. Before lunch I break to walk with the cats down a path by the plum grove to fetch the mail, shared over a midday meal with Thea. The afternoon is my best writing time. My intention is to exercise before dinner. I like to read in the evening and retire by midnight.

That's the plan, and it sometimes happens that way. But endless disruptions poke their noses in. The telephone. The voluminous mail, with its gifts and pleas, many of which deserve a proper response but usually get postcards. And the dreaded e-mail. Never was there a more mixed blessing. These electroglyphs storm my hideaway, more abundant than raindrops, more insistent than the cats at feeding time, often more vacuous than talk radio. Like its evil twin, the internet, this insidious medium consumes writing time more ravenously than anything outside an incandescent screen.

Next comes all the incidental writing—book reviews, blurbs, forewords, comments on manuscripts sent by hopeful writers, guest editorials, periodical assignments, and so on. A writer can only attend to so many of these and still write what most matters, let alone pay the bills. Speaking of which, preparation and travel for talks and teaching engagements is all time spent not writing. Add activism. Politically, I try to be reasonably informed and vote right, but perforce tune much of it out. For this I am apologetic; but knowing my limitations, unrepentant. Overlay filing; curating archives including family papers for which I am keeper; maintaining an old wooden farmhouse in a climate that receives ten to fifteen feet of rain per year, three acres threatening daily to be engulfed by Himalayan blackberry and English ivy, and a middle-aged, ex-athlete's body, while reserving something for family, friends, and community, and you have a day with significant competition for writing.

And what of reading? No one can ever "catch up," so we become reconciled to A Few Good Books. But the house fills with ephemera and serials from scientific journals to newspapers to literary magazines. Books by the cartload line the walls one and two deep. One is constantly asked to read the work of others, to judge, to commend, to edit. Against this tide only small gains can be made. Yet reading is as much a part of the work as the writing itself. It must be guarded zealously and indulged immoderately.

Finally comes the real work. When people imagine a writer's life, they sometimes picture a permanent retreat—cogitating and writing, day in, day out, all day long. The reality is that the writing often comes last in line, until the stark presence of the deadline forces the rest into the background. It is amazing to me, sometimes, that any book ever gets finished. And when it does, the author wails, like

Melville in the voice of Ishmael: "This whole book is but a draught—nay, but the draught of a draught. Oh, Time, Strength, Cash, and Patience!"

Not that when the book is done, it is done. Books are high-maintenance items, if you want them read. After the draft of the draft comes the revision, sometimes many times. *The Thunder Tree* took six years and seven drafts to balance the narrative, worldly detail, local history, place, and self. After acceptance comes edited text, then page proofs to correct, and, eventually, a book. Even then, parental care has just begun. There is the promotional tour, if budgeted. After touring big independent bookstores, I try to do a second, shoestring tour of numerous small independents around the West. This peregrination helps to keep my books where my readers are most likely to find them. Other readings and signings occur at book and author fairs, conferences, and events throughout the life of the book, but only if you arrange them. A writer must be a constant champion for the book, lest it fall from sight. And when it falls from sight anyway, you go for life after death—humping around remainders, which you must bid for, pay for, and peddle. Eventually you may recover the rights and sell the book all over again in a resurrected edition, probably just as you are finishing a new book. I've found that keeping my books available is a job of life-long shepherding—just as for any parent.

It seems to me that all this scribbling is a little pointless if it doesn't lead to real connection: connection with my own kind, and with the world at large. I am not a writer in order to be a monk, or to take part in some rarefied "process." I want to know that my efforts are worth something to someone—that they might actually affect other lives. After all, I am inept at most of the skills that make the world work. Unlike my friends and neighbors, I produce neither meat nor milk; I neither fix nor sell anything of practical value, and all the wood I log goes on my own fire. My life is bound by paper, marks on paper, and their electronic equivalents. I have exempted myself from both the tedium and the satisfaction of professional handwork in favor of mindwork. As an independent scholar and artist, have I any standing here?

Now and then, I receive dispatches from the field suggesting this work is not entirely hermetic. Letters from readers affected by my words are one of the sweetest gratifications of writing. And there are few more rewarding professional tasks than facing a roomful of people assembled to hear my work, knowing that some will take it home and read more for themselves, or perhaps to a lover or a child.

When young butterfly enthusiasts tell me that my field guide cracked open the world for them, the way F. M. Brown's *Colorado Butterflies* did for me, I am humbled and thrilled. And I am astonished how frequently readers *of The Thunder Tree* share stories of their own beloved (and usually lost) special places, and the ways in which the book brought back their importance, smell, and feel. Forest and range managers have written to thank me for giving them succor in sticking to responsible but unpopular positions, and one Bureau of Land Management agent wrote to tell me that I had changed his out-look altogether. Successive paperback editions of *Wintergreen* have been useful at Evergreen State College, where many kinds of classes have adopted it as a text over the years. And Thea's former English teacher told me how a hardback copy of *Wintergreen* had come in handy during a desert trip. I wondered if that message from the damp land had kept him moisturized in the aridlands. "No," he said, "but it made the perfect jack stand when we got stuck in the sand."

It was also *Wintergreen* that caused my most memorable reader response. Answering a knock at the back door soon after publication, I found two loggers, still in their work clothes—pegged-off jeans, red suspenders, caulk (pronounced cork) boots, hard hats. The fact that they'd left their chain saws in their rig was a good sign, but I was still unsure of their intentions. *Wintergreen,* after all, was highly critical of certain logging practices that had hurt the woods as well as the people of the woods. One asked me if my name was Powell, and I looked over my shoulder. "Did you write that book *Evergreen*?" asked the other. There was no denying that I was their boy.

I nodded, and waited for the other cork to fall. "Well, we want to buy a couple of 'em," said the first logger, "and have you sign 'em."

For several years I have been fortunate to take part in the Orion Society's Forgotten Language Tour. This is a constantly re-sorting band of gypsy writers, prank-sters, and scribblers, nature lovers all, rambling in an on-again, off-again barnstorming minstrelsy from town to town, delivering a highly movable feast of words to this region or that. I always feel, in these travels with generous friends to homeplaces where literature seems to be wanted, an astonishing sense of privilege and validation.

And when I am at home, I meet with a local writers' group—an equally intimate and loving community based in a common place, with roots deep in the timber-fish-and-farming culture of Finnish immigrants, yet with hearts and minds open enough to include a latter-day immigrant such as I. The group of seven has met monthly for the better part of a decade, sharing poems, stories, essays, meals, criticism, annual trips, and dramatically different lives that come together over the love of land and language and what they can do together.

Both of these congeries of writers are family to me, as important as anything I have written about, for it is among them that I feel the sweet, warm, and heady sense of common purpose: the shared hope of forging precious metal from the basest of materials—ordinary experience and plain language—and somehow improving the world with it.

When I find myself whining about time, it is good to look in on other lives and see how the alchemy can occur even under heavy labor. My friends do hard work in the woods, on a farm, in a family, or at a university, and then write; or go to a day job, then to school, then run an ambulance, and still write. Everyone with anything going on is equally busy. The word "busy" lacks meaning, and I have tried to banish it from my lexicon, along with the term "should." The words that do mean will somehow get written if the caring is keen enough, never mind the tyranny of time or the press of other work.

This may be where the connection that matters finally resides: in acceptance of the fact that all the work is good work if it attends to the world and the needs of people. And since one of people's greatest needs today is to relearn how to attend to the world, honest nature writing must be more than an excuse for spending time pleasantly. It must indeed be a way to forge connection, not only for ourselves, but for anyone whose citified, dried-out rootwad needs tamping down in rich, moist, solid ground.

More and more I care about writing fiction and poetry as well as the essays that have been my main work. The poems spring from the same sources and sometimes run deeper and further than the prose. Short stories are ways to explore things that *could* happen, after spending so much time and effort on things that have. And my long-term novel, *Magdalena Mountain,* is the stew into which I have been stirring the elements of art and science that together fertilize my life. On that pointy, stony place, where the black butterflies course over the high windy ridges in search of nectar, grass, and one another, I will continue to seek that symbiosis of story and natural history that finally defines every life there ever was.

On most of my meetings with Magdalena, I have

carried an implement that has become second nature to my hands, a big butterfly net named Marsha. The name came from a good college friend whose qualities—long and lithe, strong, supple, agile—seemed to apply. The pole came from a cottonwood on the High Line Canal, near the Thunder Tree itself. My brother Howard had found the branch and fashioned a walking staff from it. Returning to Colorado one summer in need of a new net, I commandeered the pole and made it into Marsha, with a broad hoop and a gossamer net bag. I took Marsha back to Gothic, where I used her to net the Magdalena alpine and other high country rarities, as I studied their ecology and behavior.

Marsha has had a hard life. That summer, on my twenty-seventh birthday, I climbed up to an eagle's aerie on Mt. Gothic. When a thunderstorm came up the valley, I cast Marsha down the mountainside so as not to have her metal hoop in my hand as lightning struck way too close. Her pole splintered at the base from impact with granite. Through years of use as an alpenstock, Marsha incurred various other injuries that I repaired with duct tape and wire. Then during my travels with monarch butterflies one recent fall, I pushed aside a recalcitrant Russian olive branch with Marsha's shaft and broke it in half. A good friend, Ed Maxwell, cleverly repaired her with marine rope-work and a copper ferrule, and she looked great. But last summer, during a field course in the Siskiyous of southwest Oregon, I stupidly left Marsha atop Thea's truck on the way to a habitat destination. As I began teaching, netless, Thea went back to retrieve her. When she returned, she was in tears. "Marsha's gone," she said.

"Lost?" I asked.

"No," she said. "Really gone." Marsha had come off on a busy highway, and had been shattered and twisted by logging trucks driving over her brittle cottonwood body, metal hoop, and net. I had to cauterize my feelings for the remainder of the seminar. Afterward, Thea and I combed the sordid debris of the roadside for bits and pieces. Not until our third pass, the following morning, did I discover that sundered base of the pole from the lightning-aerie a quarter century before, now severed. Back home, surveying the mangled wood pile that was Marsha, I felt as Barbara Drake had in a poem about a new cooking pot that she had carelessly scorched. "Oh, I am so ashamed," her poem concludes.

Friends commiserated but accused me of overweaning sentimentality for inanimate objects. I knew I "should" simply buy a nice new aluminum net from BioQuip, like the ones many of my friends use. Instead, I spent evenings glueing the bits back together as best I could. I found some good fits, but this was cottonwood, not oak, and badly splintered. There were big gaps in the fabric of the pole. I figured the best I could do was to assemble a feeble mock-up that could stand in the corner of my study as a reminder of our former field trips together, and a reproach to my forgetfulness.

I was afraid to show Ed what I'd done to his handiwork. But he took Marsha in hand for several months. Tonight he brought her back. I could not believe what he had wrought, with mortice and tenon, epoxy, sandpaper, skilled toolwork, and stains. Marsha looked almost the same, but with a handsome maculation from the filled and polished pebble dents and tire abrasions. The effect reminded me of spalted maple. Even the original crook in the handle where my hand fits perfectly, and the patina from many years of sweat and friction, were preserved. The major difference, aside from the subtly vermiculated matrix, was that Marsha is stronger than ever. I have already used her, on this warm and windy-wet November night, to catch and release a big caddis fly from an autumn hatch, trapped by a vacant spider web outside the kitchen window.

Catch-and-release is mostly what I do with Marsha, anymore, and I am thrilled that she will be with me for another season of it, come spring. And for many more beyond. The pursuit of butterflies on their high, wild trajectories is not, after all, unlike the chase after thoughts and impressions and the wily words to express them. And mending Marsha, the piecing together of a functioning whole from what seems to be utterly inadequate materials, has much in common with the preposterous presumption of one who would reassemble some part of the actual world in a book.

Next summer I hope to find the scarlet-and-jet Gillette's checkerspot, which has always eluded me, in the Montana marsh behind a friend's cabin. In the fall I will be back in the milkweed patches of the Columbia Basin, chasing monarchs and tagging them to learn where they go. In between, I hope to return to the high ridges where *Erebia magdalena* flies. Marsha may briefly hold the black butterfly in the diaphanous folds of her net. And with luck and grace, I might find that secret pass—usually hidden under snow—between the territories of what we may truly know, and what we can only hope to feel.

Robert Michael Pyle

A PORTRAIT

by Scott Slovic

Bouncing, laughing, speaking, speaking, laughing, bouncing. I carry in my mind an image of sheer delight: the literary naturalist at play and at work. It is difficult to tell where one realm leaves off and the other begins. The effort to mesh words and world is an enterprise so profoundly playful and profoundly serious that the normal distinction between avocation and vocation vanishes.

Bouncing. The lepidopterist enters the realm of the airborne darters and drifters through any means available, using net to restrain for a closer view and pen to describe, using a minitrampoline for the small gift of releasing the physical self into space one moment at a time.

Laughing. The naturalist wears a smile of satisfaction. The world is a wonderful place, dazzling. As Harry Middleton once put it, "The earth is enough." The pale gray of this century-old farmhouse in southwestern Washington contrasts with the verdant tangle of intricate greens, and in the center of the scene the learned lyricist bounces on an exercise trampoline out on the porch near a writing table. He holds small weights in his hands. He bounces and laughs. This is how the mind takes flight, literally.

Speaking. The man is a word prodigy, loquacious and adoring. Even midbounce, the monologue continues. Jokes and insights, knowledge and nonsense. The world is a wonderful mesh of meanings, and language the medium through which we attach ourselves to the bigger picture.

Speaking . . . and writing. In public or private, language is potentially a way to connect, to hold together community. "This is how it all works," says the teacher. "And what we don't understand, we explore in this way. Here, watch me." When the speaker commits words to print, the audience—suddenly abstract—expands exponentially. The possibilities of communication are astonishing. So many sparks of inspiration, so much knowledge and pleasure to share.

Laughing. Dourness does not fit the delightfulness of experience. Amidst a devoured landscape and a diminished planet, there's still so much to celebrate. For instance, you and I here, together, today— this is enough. Let's talk and bounce and laugh.

Bouncing. We feel compelled to reach for what we do not have, for what we are not. "I want, I want," exclaims the small human figure in the Blake engraving, climbing a ladder from earth to moon, arms outstretched. "I want." The literary naturalist bounces on his trampoline in the heart of the temperate rainforest of the Pacific Northwest, dreaming of a svelte physique, dreaming of words that will bear the wonder, dreaming of a mind that might approach the intricacies of complex ecosystems, dreaming of reforested Willapa Hills. What could be more out of reach than the very flight of butterflies and moths, those bright-colored and evanescent emblems of the world's subtle brilliance? And what could be more noble than to reach, bouncing and laughing and speaking, toward such brilliance?

Robert Michael Pyle came to the attention of many readers of literary natural history with the publication of *Wintergreen: Rambles in a Ravaged Land* in 1986. While he has published many books and articles since, this early volume continues to represent much of what he aims to explain as a writer: the *push* and *pull* between the outdoor life of the naturalist and the work of the writer indoors, the pain of loss and the pleasure of what remains, the vigor of the world and the mirroring vigor of words. Here is how the book begins.

> One day late last autumn, I abandoned my rural retreat for an afternoon's book work in the nearest city. Winter was closing in as I viewed the first of November from the warm, dry interior of the Longview Public Library. An autumnal confetti of leaves blew across the green, from the oaks and maples beside the art-deco post office to the stoop of the neocolonial Monticello Hotel. Cold air fell out of a low sky the color of old aluminum, pulled itself up before hitting

the ground, then raced along the sidewalk as a bitter wind. Cars squirted along the wet road with yellow leaves plastered to their windshields, while the few walkers on the scene hastened toward indoors. Mellow fall, seemingly spooked by Halloween's howling airs, was clearly in retreat.

The thing one must realize about southwestern Washington is that "wintergreen" refers merely to the greenest season in a very green place. Spring green, summer green, and autumnal green in Gray's River and environs would also boggle the eyes and imaginations of most city dwellers and noncoastal people. As Pyle writes on the final page of the book, "Green drips into deeper green." The onset of winter wetness in the Pacific Northwest implies the opportunity to savor what is essentially wonderful about that place—the pervasive water (in the air, on the ground, in the rivers and ponds) that supports all of the green life and turns the mind inward to take stock and reflect. The opening of *Wintergreen* signals that the author has "abandoned" his usual haven of the outdoors for a season of inwardness. This is, of course, the story of the naturalist's life, the rhythmic alternation of observation and reflection.

How to come to terms with what we have at hand and what we desire? When to accept and when to seek? One of the ironies of the author's choice of residences is that he's a lepidopterist in country that's "a great place for snails, one of the worst regions in the world for butterflies." "Now," he writes, "as an author of several butterfly books, I am often asked variations on the question 'What's a nice lepidopterist like you doing in a butterfly dump like this?'" In the chapter "I, Clodius," he attempts to explain. The naturalist need not always seek the richest region in order to enjoy his chief foci of fascination. In fact, the opportunity to focus one's attention may be enhanced by the paucity of specimens. This notion is profoundly linked to one of the important themes of the entire book, and of the rest of the author's work: the value of learning from and celebrating even diminished landscapes and natural systems, and yet without calmly accepting gratuitous exploitation and degradation. As I've walked with the author in various landscapes over the years, I've noticed his well-honed ability to focus on local phenomena and single specimens, from wind patterns at Great Sand Dunes National Monument in Colorado to toad carcasses on a gravel road near Nevada's Pyramid Lake. There's a photograph on my wall of the author holding a dried, flattened toad with two hands before his eager face. "What's this? How wonderful!"

Despite the scarcity of butterflies in the Willapa Hills, there is a wealth of "Waterproof Wildlife," as the next chapter explains. Salamanders, newts, toads, and frogs, otters, muskrats, beavers, nutrias, and raccoons, and birds ranging from swallows to vultures—there is, despite the previous chapter's reveling in butterfly poverty, an abundance of wild creatures living in southwestern Washington, alternately trying to stay dry and get wet.

The section "Hands on the Land" comes next. Having spent the first half of the book cultivating the reader's appreciation for the ecological richness of this humble landscape, the author turns next to reveal, with barely submerged rage, "The Sack of the Woods." This chapter tells the story of the author's efforts to save an unlogged hillside that stood on the opposite side of the Gray's River valley when he moved there in the late 1970s. His mistake: writing a letter to the timber company and calling attention to these standing trees.

> The very fact that I wrote the letter shows my callowness when I came here. I must have thought they were honorable men, these timber bosses. The loggers I knew were not only honorable but likable. Tutored at two forestry schools in the romance of the early logging days and the righteousness of modern industrial sustained-yield forestry and determined not to let my environmentalist bias get in the way of good relations with my neighbors, I somehow expected more of the company. There is that in goodwill that expects reciprocity. When it doesn't come, when you extend your hand and get kicked in the face—that's when you wonder.

Even as he tells the story of this particular outrage, Pyle's beef remains with the big companies, with Crown Zellerbach and Weyerhaeuser, not with individual loggers. Still, it was an act of notable personal risk even to write about the transgressions of the timber companies. Since the appearance of *Wintergreen,* nearly a decade and a half ago, naturally there has been some suspicion of the author. Log trucks' noisy airbrakes often blow as the drivers round the curve on the state highway above his home. The jake breaks may be normal, or they may mean "hello," or perhaps some other salute. Although he has had one or two tense encounters with locals since the book came out, the menace, he believes, lies in the mindless greed of the corporations, not in the average men in the woods.

In her recent book *Ecology of a Cracker Childhood,* Janisse Ray writes, "In south Georgia everything is flat and wide. Not empty. My people live among the mobile homes, junked cars, pine plantations, clearcuts, and fields." Her book offers a kind of junkyard ecology, ranging from memories of a rough-and-tumble childhood among the small-town poor in the American South to explanations of the subtle, remaining natural species and systems in the region. Likewise, *Wintergreen* offers a "stump-field ecology," a wry effort to come to terms with the remaining wild vitality of old forest clear-cuts. In the elegiac chapter "Stump Watcher," logged-over hillsides are presented as loci of meaningful life, not as desecrated temples:

> For a naturalist living in a land of logging, compensation must be sought for the daily, depressing vista of endless clearcuts; solace for the melancholic thought of great forests that are no

more. For me, one such payment comes in the form of the very things the loggers saw fit to leave behind: those mossy, rotting, wonderful stumps.

"Mossy, rotting, wonderful stumps." What kind of nature writing is this, celebrating a ravaged landscape? Having expressed his anger and frustration in earlier chapters, Pyle here signals his return to ingenuous, unironic celebration and fascination, his more comfortable modes of expression. There is no coyness and irony in this concluding statement of pleasure about the fecundity of tree stumps. This is a wonder: that life should spring forth so enthusiastically from devastation.

The celebratory conclusion of "Stump Watcher" leads smoothly to the concluding section of *Wintergreen,* entitled "Out of the Mists." The chapter "Rain-Forest Year" is a virtuoso rhapsody about rain and fog, a joyous acknowledgment of the very features of the Pacific Northwest that drive many a visitor to the region back home again, exclaiming, "Too rainy, too gloomy, too gray." Not so for Pyle, who finds in the 120 or so inches of rain received each year in the Willapa woods much to love. The chapter offers a seasonal cycle of "page-pictures," apparently drawn from the author's journal. The lushness of the language in these sketches mirrors the verdant landscape. Take one of the January paragraphs, for instance:

> January, most years, sees the falling of the heaviest rains. Then the world seems truly awash in

Willapa. But it can also bring high pressure off the ocean, and with it, flirting interstices of sunshine. No matter how often they occur, the wet, gray lambasts always bring a sense of persecution, and the sun-running balmy days lend a feeling of unseasonable privilege. But whether January speaks in sunbeams or rainbows, or merely mumbles through the mossehurr, the month has a lingua franca in mist. Bright days and cloudy too usually dawn with fog. A nuisance to many, fog to me is more palliative than pall.

Naturalists, in general, may be a breed apart, especially in this day and age. But Pyle is a breed apart from most naturalists, so cheerful can he be even amidst the damp gray that so well suits the name of his Gray's River home. It may be relatively easy to love nature when one is in the crystal air of the Rocky Mountains or feeling the gentle trade winds of the tropics. To say, sincerely, that the coastal Northwest's ever-present winter fog is "more palliative than pall" takes special affection . . . some would say gall.

The essay "And the Coyotes Will Lift a Leg," the book's penultimate chapter, begins with a sustained meditation on the saying, Nature bats last. "What does it mean?" asks Pyle.

It means, we may be in the lead now, the natural world may seem the underdog and down in points as well. But when we've finished our act, hit the grand slam, or struck out (which may be the same thing), nature has an extra inning coming—all to herself, unopposed, unending. No one will be keeping score anymore, and guess who wins?

Cosmic history as a baseball game. Well, this is a rather glum projection, is it not? Pyle begs to differ, insisting that his happiness is undeterred by this sober vision.

> An ungenerous reader could mutter "Cynic!" and close the book, so near the end. But I am not cynical about humans and the rest of nature. When I insist upon the mortality of all species, including our own, it is not an unhappy thought. And when I invoke that aphorism of uncertain category and origin, "nature bats last," it is in good cheer that I do so. My outlook, ultimately, is not a pessimistic one. But then my frame of reference does not encompass human fortunes alone.

As *Wintergreen* wends its way toward the end, the stump-watcher and lepidopterist emerges as cheerful inhumanist, his version of the tradition as jocular as the jabs of Edward Abbey—"I'd rather kill a *man* than a snake"—but perhaps sweeter. "Cosmic optimism" is what Pyle calls this state of mind. Not a bad psychological tendency to have when one lives in a gray country, a lover of wild woods surrounded by clear-cut gashes.

"Wintergreen" is the final chapter of the book,

pulling the volume to a close in a gesture of symmetry that pleases Pyle's sense of order.

> I began this book by describing an early winter's day as viewed within the warmth of the Longview Public Library. Just a year later, I found myself in the same chair whence that picture originated, entering winter once more. We seek symmetry and continuity in our lives. In finishing these essays where they began, I felt a pleasing sense of both.

The abiding themes of the chapter are "rot, decay, senescence," a seemingly dark way to end what had been such a celebratory tour of Willapa. There are, indeed, flickers of fear and even rage, but through it all, from amidst the direness, comes celebration of vital, organic richness, from the exuberance of exploding sword ferns to the tropical spread of hemlocks, growing from clear-cut stumps.

Symmetry and angularity; graceful repetitions and abrupt shifts. Robert Michael Pyle has known the processes of change and disruption his entire life, and his sanguine, peaceful demeanor belies a deep familiarity with loss. At the same time, his life has been blessed with uncanny returns and recurrences, with extraordinary continuity in a discordant world.

Robert Harold Pyle, the author's father, was born in Carlisle County, Kentucky, in 1914 to parents who divorced sometime in the 1920s. Helen Lee Miller was born in 1916 in Seattle, Washington; her parents divorced in the 1930s. Robert H. Pyle and Helen Miller's marriage in Denver, Colorado, in 1939, lasted until 1956, when Helen moved back to Seattle. While they were together, they had four children: Susan Leslie Pyle (now Kafer) was born in 1941, followed by Thomas Edward Pyle in 1943. Robert Michael Pyle was born on July 19, 1947, in Denver. His younger brother, Howard Whetstone Pyle, was born in 1952.

Pyle and his family lived in North Denver until 1953, when they moved to Hoffman Heights in the nearby town of Aurora. His father worked for Mutual Office Supply Company in Denver. When Pyle was six years old, just beginning to attend Peoria Elementary School, his grandmother, Nancy Lois Cannon Pyle, died of cancer in Denver at the age of fifty-eight. Known in those years as "Bobby," Pyle began frequenting the High Line Canal in Aurora, and it was in 1954 that the tremendous hailstorm later documented in his book *The Thunder Tree* occurred. He also began collecting shells that year.

Four years later, at the age of eleven, in the wake of his parents' divorce, he began collecting butterflies, inspired by a *National Geographic* article called "Butterflies—Try and Get Them!" His father remarried in 1959, and it was during a visit to his stepmother's family cabin in Crested Butte, Colorado, that the junior high school student met distinguished ecologists Charles Remington and Paul Ehrlich at the Rocky Mountain Biological Laboratory in the silver-mining ghost town of Gothic. Nearly twenty years later, Remington would serve as Pyle's Ph.D. mentor at Yale University and back at Gothic.

Pyle's mother left her second husband in 1960 and moved to Pueblo, Colorado, returning a year later to the Hoffman Heights home and assuming custody of Bob and his brothers. Susan, by this time, was a student at Colorado State College. A ninth grader at South Junior High, Bob met his future wife, JoAnne Clark, in 1961. From 1962 to 1965, he attended Aurora Central High School, and during these years he received a National Science Foundation precollege grant to spend the summer of 1963 at Jackson Memorial Laboratory in Bar Harbor, Maine, and a Colorado-Wyoming Academy of Science grant for wood nymph butterfly research the following summer. Bob and JoAnne, by then engaged, matriculated together at the University of Washington in the fall of 1965 and were married a year later. Distracted and unenthused by the standard curriculum, Bob nearly flunked out of Washington before turning his attention to birding and natural history classes. He became active with the Conservation Education and Action Council (CEAC) at the university in 1967 and wrote a number of advocacy articles—his first publications—during the mid-1960s with such titles as "Don't Dam(n) It—Save It!" and "Discover an Urban Sanctuary—Then Save It!" and "Conservation and the Lepidopterist." From the beginning, his literary and scientific lives were intertwined with a devotion to conservation issues, an awareness of the political side of writing and natural history. The year 1967 marked more loss, as his mother died at the age of fifty-two. But he also met Thea Linnaea Peterson, who would become his third wife in 1985, in a mycology class at the university.

In 1969, Pyle began studying nature interpretation with Professor Grant W. Sharpe, which led to the creation of an independent major in nature perception and protection. He spent the summer of that year working as a ranger-naturalist in California's Sequoia National Park. The experience of leading a CEAC march to take over and reclaim the Union Bay Fill/Marsh on the university campus led to a high-profile essay called "Union Bay: A Life-after-death Plant-in," published side-by-side with N. Scott Momaday's "An American Land Ethic" in *Ecotactics: The Sierra Club Handbook for Environmental Activists*. Bob completed his B.S. at Washington in 1970 and promptly entered the master's program in the university's College of Forest Resources, with an emphasis on nature interpretation. That summer, JoAnne became a ranger-naturalist at Katmai National Monument in Alaska, while Bob held several interpretive jobs in Washington. After his brother Howard ("Bud") sustained a major head injury in an automobile accident in northeastern Oregon, Bob spent much of the summer there. While awaiting Bud's slow recovery at a LaGrande hospital, he photographed butterflies in nearby canyons for his master's thesis.

Pyle spent 1971–1972 on a Fulbright-Hays Scholarship at the Monks Wood Experimental Station outside of Cambridge, England. There he worked with John Heath on rare butterfly conservation studies. This research inspired Pyle to establish the Xerces Society for invertebrate conservation on December 9, 1971, an organization which has become an important force for conservation among the international scientific community, publishing the biannual journal *Wings: Essays on Invertebrate Conservation*. Drifting apart for professional and geographic reasons, he and JoAnne were amicably divorced in Seattle in 1973, although they remain good friends. Pyle completed his M.S. at Washington that spring and moved to New Haven, Connecticut, to begin the Ph.D. program in the School of Forestry and Environmental Studies, where he worked with renowned population biologist Charles L. Remington, whom he first met in 1959. Throughout these early years of graduate school, Pyle was publishing many essays on natural history and environmental protection in magazines and journals ranging from *Seattle Audubon Notes* to the *Journal of the Lepidopterists' Society*. By the time he entered Yale, he had published nearly forty articles.

The Seattle Audubon Society published Pyle's first book, *Watching Washington Butterflies*, in 1974. This guidebook was a modified version of his master's thesis. He also began to write a novel, *Magdalena Mountain*, that year, a project that has continued to the present. He and Sarah Anne ("Sally") Hughes married in Bath, England, and moved to the Rocky Mountain Biological Laboratory to do research. In 1975, Pyle paid visits to Edwin Way Teale and Roger Tory Peterson at their Connecticut homes, realizing that his own future as a writer might well lead him in the direction of their natural history works for popular audiences. At the same time, he was immersed in technical research for his Ph.D. dissertation titled *The Eco-Geographic Basis for Lepidoptera Conservation,* which he completed in 1976. Sally began graduate work in Museum Studies at the University of Leicester, and Bob moved with her to England, where he taught writing and conservation at the Vale of Catmose Village College in Rutland.

Having completed his doctorate, Pyle began searching for university teaching positions, but could not find an appropriate permanent position; from 1976 to the present, he has held a variety of part-time and visiting professorships in creative writing, natural history, and conservation biology at such institutions as Lewis & Clark College, Evergreen State College, Portland State University, and the Rocky Mountain Biological Laboratory. From 1977 to 1979, he worked as a butterfly conservation consultant for the Wildlife Department of Papua New Guinea, and the National Academy of Science. At the same time, when not traveling, he worked as the Northwest Land Steward for The Nature Conservancy, based out of Portland, Oregon. Although he continued to live a rather itinerant existence as a conservation consultant, Pyle found and bought his home (called "Swede Park") in Gray's River, Washington, in 1978. He visited such far-flung places as Turkmenia and Kenya for the International Union for Conservation of Nature and Natural Resources General Assembly, and in 1979 and 1980 divided his time between Gray's River, Costa Rica, and Cambridge, England, while creating an Invertebrate Red Data Book and comanaging the Species Conservation Unit of IUCN/ WWF, based in Cambridge. He began his association with the Orion Society in 1980 as well, writing a column called "Niche of a Naturalist" for *Orion* magazine. At this time he was also working on *The Audubon Society Field Guide to North American Butterflies,* which was published by Knopf in 1981 and remains in print nearly twenty years later. Another major personal loss occurred in 1980 with the death of his father in Denver, from lung cancer, at the age of sixty-six.

When a house fire occurred at Swede Park while Pyle was in Cambridge in 1982, he returned home to Washington State and decided to stay, thus beginning what he calls his "freelance existence." The following year, he published his first of many books with Houghton Mifflin, beginning his longtime association with editor Harry Foster; this initial Houghton Mifflin volume was the *Peterson Field Guide to Butterflies Coloring Book.* But even as his professional life began to sort itself out, Pyle's private life continued to shift and change; he and Sally were divorced in Seattle in 1983 and she returned to England. One of the unique things about Pyle's personal relationships is that he has maintained close friendships with both JoAnne and Sally following their divorces.

In 1984, Scribner published the *Handbook for Butterfly Watchers.* In his foreword, Roger Tory Peterson claims, "Perhaps no one has done more to popularize butterfly watching than Robert Pyle, author of this handbook. . . . There is no doubt that butterfly watching is fun, but we must thank [Pyle] for pointing the way and giving us tips so that our butterfly observations might be more meaningful." Indeed, this handbook, like Pyle's other popular butterfly writings, is notable for its combination of biological detail, simple and practical advice for both novice butterfly watchers and aficionados, lively anecdotes, and ingenuous enthusiasm for butterflies and natural history in general. Although it's called a handbook, this publication reads like a work of literature, and this is, in fact, the overarching goal of Pyle's writing. As he told Ray Kelleher for a 1996 interview in *Poet's & Writers Magazine,*

> The real question is: is it literary or not? Is it personal? Does it follow a discovering line? Does it digress, wander, and explore? Does it have the presumption of objectivity, or does it respect the writer as a lens that will refract? That's the joy of the essay—when the writer becomes the subjective lens—and it's the same joy in fiction and poetry.

Pyle's readiness to bring his literary vision into scientific work and scientific observation into the literary realm—indeed, his unwillingness to acknowledge any incompatibility between the two modes of thinking and expression—is an essential aspect of his professional life.

Bob's old friend, Thea (Peterson) Hellyer, joined

him at Swede Park in 1984. The two were married at home a year later, and Thea's children, thirteen-year-old Tom and ten-year-old Dory, came to live with them. It was in these happy circumstances that Bob's breakthrough literary work, *Wintergreen*, came to fruition. As he mentions in his acknowledgments, Thea not only read and commented on the entire manuscript, but she made the line drawing of single-flowered wintergreens for the title page, the first of her title page drawings that have since graced all of Bob's books. Biographers have noted that Thea, Tom, and Dory helped to give Bob a stable, orderly family structure for the first time in his adult life. Jane Elder Wulff, in a profile for the regional *Peninsula Magazine*, observes that Thea, herself a botanist and silkscreen artist, nicely balances Bob's temperament: "Thea runs the house so Bob can work. . . . Their personalities are complementary. She rises early, goes for a run along the pastoral back roads around Gray's River, and wakes her husband at midmorning with breakfast in the upstairs bedroom overlooking the valley." Pyle often begins the day composing in bed, looking out the window at the valley, while Thea gardens or works in her studio.

Wintergreen, published in hardcover, appeared to great acclaim in 1986 from Scribner. The book was recognized in 1987 with the John Burroughs Medal for outstanding natural history writing, the Governor's Writers Award, and the Pacific Northwest Booksellers Association Award, and then the hardcover edition was promptly shredded by Macmillan (the company that had acquired Scribner) due to less than stellar sales. Fortunately, Houghton Mifflin brought out the paperback edition a year later (with the new subtitle, *Listening to the Land's Heart*), just as Pyle began working on his next literary project, *The Thunder Tree,* under Harry Foster's editorial guidance. Even as he continued to draft and polish *The Thunder Tree,* he applied for and received a Guggenheim grant to begin the cryptozoological study of Sasquatch, an adventure in the natural and cultural history of one of the most famous and most marginal of Pacific Northwest environmental topics. The actual trek to the Dark Divide region of southcentral Washington, to conduct Bigfoot research, took place throughout the autumn of 1990. When not writing or out in the field doing research, he also continued his environmental service during these years, having been appointed to the Natural Heritage Advisory Council in 1989.

One of Pyle's most important social and literary activities involves his participation in a local writers' group in the Gray's River area, a group that he helped to found in 1992. Much of his own writing since then has first been shared with friends in the group.

In 1993, *The Thunder Tree* appeared from Houghton Mifflin, recounting Pyle's boyhood in suburban Denver. This volume is significant, in part, because it joins the important tradition of urban American writing about nature, along with such classics as John Kieran's 1959 volume *Natural History of New York City* and more recent publications such as the Los Angeles section of John McPhee's *The Control of Nature* and Robert Sullivan's *The Meadowlands: Wilderness Adventures at the Edge of a City.* In a key chapter, "The Extinction of Experience," Pyle identifies the ominous implications of modern urban life:

> The extinction of experience is not just about losing the personal benefits of the natural high. It also implies a cycle of disaffection that can have disastrous consequences. As cities and metastasizing suburbs forsake their natural diversity, and their citizens grow more removed from personal contact with nature, awareness and appreciation retreat. This breeds apathy toward environmental concerns and, inevitably, further degradation of the common habitat.

Although *The Thunder Tree,* too, enjoyed only a short shelf life in hardcover before being remaindered, it was picked up by The Lyons Press in 1998 and reprinted in paperback. Just as *The Thunder Tree* first appeared, Pyle was becoming actively involved in various Orion Society projects, attending the first John Hay Award event on Cape Cod and a year later participating in one of the first Forgotten Language tours (the Orion Society's multistop reading tour for environmental writers). He would begin writing a column called "Tangled Bank" in 1997 for the Society's publication devoted to community activism, *Orion Afield.*

In 1994, he joined discussions of *Nabokov's Butterflies,* a collection of Vladimir Nabokov's scientific and literary butterfly writings, with Deanne

Urmy at Beacon Press, later enlisting Nabokov's biographer Brian Boyd to coedit and annotate the book and his son Dmitri Nabokov to translate unpublished material. For a year, beginning in 1994, he also wrote the "Gray's River Almanac" column for the journal *Illahee*, published by the University of Washington's Institute for Environmental Studies before the institute was shut down after existing for nearly a quarter century, and the journal with it. In his passionate and straight-shooting final column, "Elegy Written in a Country Farmyard," Pyle quotes his own letter to the acting provost at the university, stating: "In a state, a region, a nation, and a world where environmental inquiry and informed response is the single paramount concern, your action is embarrassing, unconscionable, and wrong."

Even while engaging himself in heated conservation efforts and institutional struggles, Pyle continued working on his long-term literary projects. *Where Bigfoot Walks: Crossing the Dark Divide* appeared from Houghton Mifflin in 1995, offering a profound and playful examination not so much of Bigfoot the creature as Bigfoot the phenomenon. Still, Pyle never closes his mind to the possibility of Bigfoot's existence, and this is one of the main points of the project: that we need to preserve wild places in the world because they help us, as a species, to maintain open-mindedness and a sense of wonder. As he later said to interviewer Casey Walker,

> Can creature or landscape act as a guide, as a way beyond the vast wall of indifference and blunted sensibilities that we tend to carry

around with us? . . . Whether it's a dramatic guru such as Big Foot [sic] or a subtle, simple, humble creature such as a little butterfly, wild things know how to live. . . . If we can try clearly to see through their eyes, to experience something of what they experience without making the assumption that we ever can truly share their eptitude, it gives us firmer purchase on what is out there. And how can that be anything but good?

Its explicit focus on Bigfoot and the wilds of Washington State notwithstanding, the underlying subject of *Where Bigfoot Walks* is the far-reaching study of human imagination and attentiveness to the natural world. The presses had barely cooled after the production of the Bigfoot book when Pyle was embarking on his next research and writing project, an eight-week quest to follow the migratory movements of monarch butterflies through the western states and down to Mexico. He covered 9,462 miles in his 1982 Honda Civic, nicknamed "Powdermilk," during this journey in the fall of 1996. *Chasing Monarchs: Migrating with the Butterflies of Passage* appeared in 1999 and attempts, in the author's typical anecdotal style, to answer such questions as "Where and when and how do western monarchs migrate[?]"

At the age of fifty-two, Pyle is now as active as ever, enjoying accolades from scientific colleagues (the Society for Conservation Biology gave him its Distinguished Service Award in 1997) and recognition from conservation organizations and literary scholars. As he completes his *Credo* manuscript, he is also proofreading *Nabokov's Butterflies,* preparing *The Butterflies of Cascadia* for publication by Seattle Audubon, writing the eighth draft of *Magdalena Mountain,* drafting a new "Gray's River Book" for Houghton Mifflin, and pausing regularly to teach natural history and writing workshops and give readings from his latest publications. This is the pace that has enabled him to publish more than four hundred essays, articles, reviews, papers, columns, letters, stories, and poems during the past thirty years.

The proclivity to love the world of physical things and the proclivity to strive for eloquent language seem deeply intertwined. The intensity of Robert Michael Pyle's devotion to the physical world, to the thingness of experience, is demonstrated, in part, by his devotion to the tools of his wanderings and his writing craft. Early in his *Credo* essay, he playfully explains his radical new laptop technology, impervious to power surges and the fickleness of weather: a thick, black, ringed notebook and a collection of number two pencils, made in China. His narrative essays refer routinely to his favorite tool of all: the butterfly net named "Marsha."

Although Pyle mentions Marsha in many of his writings, the net made perhaps its most sustained appearance until now in the final chapter of *The Thunder Tree:*

> I have long carried on my summer walks a massive butterfly net respectfully named Marsha after a strong friend. My brother Bud carved it

first as a walking staff from a High Line cottonwood pole. I use it for that at least as much as for netting insects. Marsha's crook, oiled and burnished from years of use, just fits my grasp. In its strength I feel the power of all the cottonwoods.

Today the author can scarcely recall when this pole came into his life. Perhaps it was retrieved from the canal in 1968 or 1969; by 1974, certainly, it achieved its form as a butterfly net. When Bud attended one of Bob's literary readings for the first time, in October of 1999, Bob explained how Bud had "carved" the pole to shape it for the net; no, Bud countered, it had not been carved, but merely sanded down. Sanded or carved, the elegant staff has been around for a while— it has become more than an object.

Marsha has become the author's way of reaching out toward the delicate lightness of the world, his point of physical contact with beautiful, fluttering things. The net itself consists of a long pole, roughhewn like a walking stick, nearly five feet long, a substantial piece of wood that fills the hands, attached at one end to a gauzy bag, itself close to three feet deep. Marsha's mouth is a good fifteen inches in diameter. When I visited Pyle in Gray's River, I asked to hold Marsha and receive tips in her use, grasping her with two hands and sweeping the air. Pyle himself posed for a photograph with Marsha, pretending to be a Viking warrior, armed not with a spear but with the most gentle of net-tipped poles.

With the writer's pencil and the lepidopterist's net, Pyle seeks to pull the experience of the world's beauty into language. Often the results are slim: a single moth after an evening of reaching, a sentence worth keeping from pages and pages of draft manuscript. Love for the physical world, for the real, combines an appreciation for both the objects of examination and the process of engagement. I noticed in May that Marsha's handle had been glued and bound with high-strength twine a foot down from the net, and learned that "she" had once been broken—yet rather than replace the net Pyle had made a special point of restoration.

What I am building toward is an account of Marsha's eventual destruction—the tale recounted at the end of this *Credo* essay—and the writer's response. About six weeks after my visit to Gray's River, I met Pyle at a conference on the East Coast. He pulled me aside and, teary-eyed, told me about a natural history workshop he'd recently been teaching in the Siskiyous of southwest Oregon. So engaged was he in the workshop that he inadvertently left Marsha atop Thea's truck and drove onto the highway where the precious net fell off and was smashed to pieces by passing traffic. When they realized what had happened, Bob and Thea retraced their route, stopped on the highway, and collected as many of the pieces of Marsha as they could find—perhaps two hundred of them, some large and many tiny fragments. Telling me this story in June, he still did not know what would become of these pieces. It was possible that Marsha was beyond recovery, but he hoped he would somehow be able to put her back together.

Five months later, I called to inquire about Marsha's fate and to urge the author to include this story in his book. At the time, Marsha was in the able hands of Ed Maxwell, manager of local fish hatcheries, who had repaired the beloved net in the past. "He'll use some epoxy and wood filler, and Marsha will end up even stronger than before," Pyle explained. "The pieces may not all be in the original places, though."

Absurd sentimentality? A clear indication of the typical soft-headedness of the poetic sensibility? I think, rather, that this devotion to a single object that has emerged from inert thingness to become, over time, a full-fledged companion, despite its composition of wood and metal and mesh, is a remarkable indication of a mentality of engagement and commitment in the midst of our contemporary throw-away culture. The typical person in America today would not have kept an old butterfly net for a decade or longer—nor would the average person, for that matter, be spending time scanning woods and fields for butterflies, alas. The typical person, upon losing such a tool, would have fretted about the expense of replacing it and then simply bit the bullet and purchased another. An environmentally sensitive person might have retraced his steps, picked up the pieces of the demolished net, and then thrown them in the trash. The writer's attitude toward this experience is reflected in his contemplation of how to keep things intact, how to restore even what seems lost and value what is less than pristine. From Marsha the butterfly net to the High Line Canal, from the Willapa Hills to the Dark Divide, damaged and threatened objects and places have too few champions in the world. Robert Michael Pyle devotes his art and science to this work.

Bibliography of Robert Michael Pyle's Work

BOOKS

The Butterflies of Cascadia. Seattle: Seattle Audubon Society, 2000.

Chasing Monarchs: Migrating with the Butterflies of Passage. Boston: Houghton Mifflin, 1999.

Where Bigfoot Walks: Crossing the Dark Divide. Boston: Houghton Mifflin, 1995. Tokyo: Tuttle-Mori Agency, 1997 (Japanese translation).

With Kristin Kest and Roger Tory Peterson. *Insects: A Peterson Field Guide Coloring Book*. Boston: Houghton Mifflin, 1993.

The Thunder Tree: Lessons from an Urban Wildland. Boston: Houghton Mifflin, 1993. New York: Lyons Press, 1998 (paperback edition).

Wintergreen: Rambles in a Ravaged Land. New York: Charles Scribner's Sons, 1986. *Wintergreen: Listening to the Land's Heart*. Boston: Houghton Mifflin, 1988 (paperback edition). Boston: Houghton Mifflin, 1995 (second paperback edition).

The Audubon Society Handbook for Butterfly Watchers. New York: Charles Scribner's Sons, 1984. *Handbook for Butterfly Watchers*. Boston: Houghton Mifflin, 1992 (paperback edition).

With Sarah Anne Hughes and Roger Tory Peterson. *A Field Guide to the Butterflies Coloring Book.* Boston: Houghton Mifflin, 1983. (Subsequent printings titled *Butterflies: A Peterson Field Guide Coloring Book.*)

With S. M. Wells and N. M. Collins. *IUCN Invertebrate Red Data Book.* Cambridge, England: IUCN/WWF, Conservation Monitoring Centre, 1983.

The Audubon Society Field Guide to North American Butterflies. New York: Alfred A. Knopf, 1981. New York: Alfred A. Knopf, 1995 (second edition).

The Ecogeographical Basis for Lepidoptera Conservation. Ann Arbor, Mich.: University Microfilms, 1976.

Watching Washington Butterflies. Seattle: Seattle Audubon Society, 1974.

CHAPBOOKS

Essays by Robert Michael Pyle: Schoenfeldt Distinguished Writers. Portland: University of Portland, 1996.

EDITED BOOKS AND JOURNALS

Edited and annotated with Brian Boyd with translations by Dmitri Nabokov. *Nabokov's Butterflies: Unpublished and Uncollected Writings.* Boston: Beacon Press, 2000. London: Penguin Press, 2000 (British edition).

Willapa Review 1, no. 1 (1985).

Atala 9, nos. 1–2 (1981 (84)).

Atala 8, no. 2 (1980 (82)).

Atala 8, no. 1 (1980 (82)).

Atala 7, no. 2 (1979 (81)).

Atala 7, no. 1 (1979 (81)).

Atala 6, nos. 1–2 (1978 (81)).

Atala 5, no. 2 (1977).

Atala 5, no. 1 (1977).

Rutland Review (Oakham, England) 1, no. 1 (1977).

Atala 4, nos. 1–2 (1976).

Atala 3, no. 2 (Fall/Winter 1975).

Atala 3, no. 1 (Spring 1975).

Atala 2, no. 2 (December 1974).

Atala 2, no. 1 (June 1974).

Atala 1, no. 2 (December 1973).

Atala (Journal of the Xerces Society) 1, no. 1 (April 1973).

UNCOLLECTED ESSAYS AND ARTICLES

"For the Love of Monarchs." *Attaché* (August 2000).

"When Things Go Wrong." *Orion Afield* 4, no. 3 (Summer 2000): 8.

"Butterfly Releases." *Northwest Lepidopterists' Association Newsletter* (Spring 2000): 4.

"John Hinchcliff: A Reminiscence." *Northwest Lepidopterists' Association Newsletter* (Spring 2000): 4–5.

"Of Cabbages and Queens." *Orion Afield* 4, no. 2 (Spring 2000): 8.

"Ruler of a Vast Domain." *Terra* 37, no. 2 (Spring 2000): 12.

"Sky River." *Terra* 37, no. 2 (Spring 2000): 10–11, 13, 15.

"Transformations." *Terra* 37, no. 2 (Spring 2000): 14.

"Good of Grays River Community at Risk." *Longview Daily News* (March 22, 2000): A6.

"The Earth Turns, and We Go On." *Daily Astorian Commemorative Millennium Issue* (January 2000): 2.

"Declaration of Independents." *PNBA Footnotes* (January 2000): 2.

"Nabokov's Butterflies." *American Scholar* 69, no. 1 (Winter 2000): 95–110.

"Old Growth." *Wamka*, no. 5 (2000): 14.

"Down at the Grange." *Orion Afield* 4, no. 1 (Winter 1999/2000): 8.

"Monarch Butterflies." *Open Spaces* 2, no. 3 (Autumn 1999): 45–46.

"Naming Names." *Orion Afield* 3, no. 4 (Autumn 1999): 8.

"A River of Monarchs." *Portland* 18, no. 3 (Autumn 1999): 28–29.

Excerpt from *Chasing Monarchs*. *Entertainment Weekly,* no. 501 (September 3, 1999): 65.

"Turning Fifty on Silver Star." *American Hiker* 12, no. 4 (August/September 1999): 26.

Contribution to "A Sand County Celebration." *Audubon Naturalists' News* 25, no. 6 (July/August 1999): 7.

Excerpt from *Chasing Monarchs*. *American Butterflies* 7, no. 2 (Summer 1999): 32–36.

"Old Growth." *Forest Voice* 10, no. 3 (Summer 1999): 14.

"A Declaration of Independents." *Orion Afield* 3, no. 3 (Summer 1999): 8.

"The Element of Surprise." *Orion Afield* 3, no. 2 (Spring 1999): 8.

"More Than Monarchs in Central Mexico." *Monarch News* 9, no. 6 (March 1999): 6–7.

"A Declaration of Independents." *Chuckanut Review* 5, no. 4 (Winter 1999): 12–13.

"Roll Call." *Nature's Log* (Ogden, Utah) (Winter 1999): 10–11.

"Old Growth." *Orion Afield* 3, no. 1 (Winter 1999): 8.

"A Report on the Society for Ecological Restoration International Conference, Austin, Texas." *Monarch News* 9, no. 1 (October 1998): 3.

"The Tangled Bank." *Headwaters' Forest News* (Fall 1998): 35.

"In the Shadow of Jane Goodall." *Orion Afield* 2, no. 4 (Autumn 1998): 42–43.

"Roll Call." *Orion Afield* 2, no. 4 (Autumn 1998): 8.

"Natural Areas: A Common Sense Approach." *Aberdeen (Wash.) Daily World* (August 26, 1998): 4–5.

"Wedding Releases and the Community of Lepidopterists." *Monarch News* 8, no. 11 (August 1998): 1, 3.

"The Case for Natural Area Preserves." *Chinook Observer* (July 22, 1998): A5.

"Turning Fifty on Silver Star." *Orion Afield* 2, no. 3 (Summer 1998): 8.

"Correction and Comment." *Monarch News* 8, no. 7 (April 1998): 9.

"Do Butterfly Releases Interfere with Conservation?" *Monarch News* 8, no. 7 (April 1998): 8–9.

With Jeffrey Glassberg, Paul Opler, Robert Robbins, and James Tuttle. "There's No Need to Release Butterflies— They're Already Free." *American Butterflies* (Spring 1998): 2.

"The Way of the Monarch." *Great Basin* 2, no. 3 (Spring 1998): 9, 15, 23, 24, 26, 31.

"Of Mice and Monarchs." *Orion Afield* 2, no. 2 (Spring 1998): 8.

"The Biogeography of Hope: Why Transporting Butterflies Is a Bad Idea." *Monarch News* 8, no. 6 (March 1998): 6–7.

"On the Outside." *Society for Conservation Biology Newsletter* 5, no. 1 (February 1998): 1–2.

"In the Eyes of . . ." *Orion Afield* 2, no. 1 (Winter 1997/1998): 3, 6.

"Two Butterfly Backpacks." *Northwest Lepidopterists' Association Newsletter* 12, no. 3 (Fall 1997): 10.

"The Lepidoptera as a Vessel of Discovery." *Wings* 20, no. 2 (Fall 1997): 19–20.

With Thea L. Pyle. "Citizens Are Fed Up with Poisoned Roadsides." *Longview (Wash.) Daily News* (September 9, 1997): 8.

"Amazing Grace: The Migration of Monarch Butterflies." *Vermilion Flycatcher* 41, no. 9 (September 1997): 4.

"Land Notes: A Willapa Reading List." *Stonecrop* 1 (Summer 1997): 35–37.

"Amazing Grace: The Migration of Monarch Butterflies." *Earthcare Northwest* (Seattle Audubon Society) 38, no. 7 (April 1997): 6.

Commentary on Jack Turner Forum. *Wild Duck Review* 3, no. 2 (April 1997): 24.

"Burning Bridges." *Wings* 20, no. 1 (Spring 1997): 22–23.

"Natural Heritage." *Chinook Observer* (February 4, 1997): A4.

Contribution to Jack Turner Forum. *Wild Duck Review* 3, no. 1 (February 1997): 23–26.

"Leaves That Speak." *Orion Afield* 1, no. 1 (1997): 6.

"Recent Northwest Initiatives in Lepidoptera Conservation." *News of the Lepidopterists' Society* 38, no. 6 (October–December 1996): 182.

"I Was a Teenage Lepidopterist." *Portland* 15, no. 3 (Autumn 1996): 24–25.

"Author Explores Haunts of Bigfoot." *Signpost* 31, no. 9 (September 1996): 24–25.

"Back to Earth." *Wild Duck Review* 2, no. 4 (July/August 1996): 20–23.

"Elegy Written in a Country Farmyard." *Illahee* 11, nos. 3–4 (Fall/Winter 1995): 124–29.

"Parents without Children: Confessions of a Favorite Uncle." *Orion* 14, no. 4 (Autumn 1995): 26–29.

"Butterflies in Winter." *Wings* 18, no. 2 (Fall 1995): 17–21.

"Profiles of Pacific Northwest Lepidopterists: Benjamin Vilnuve Leighton, 1918–1989." *Northwest Lepidopterists' Association Newsletter,* no. 1 (Summer 1995): 3–5.

"Bigfoot Baby Found in Watermelon, Has Elvis's Sneer." *Orion* 14, no. 3 (Summer 1995): 16–23.

"Where Bigfoot Walks." *Portland* 14, no. 2 (Summer 1995): 16–19.

"Ditch, Creek, River." *Illahee* 11, nos. 1–2 (Spring/Summer 1995): 7–10.

"Ripples Through a Pool of Meltwater." *Orion Society Notebook* 1, no. 1 (Spring/Summer 1995): 4.

"A War of Ideologies, with Endangered Species as Weapons." *High Country News* 27, no. 9 (May 15, 1995): 13.

"Monsters in the Mist." *Eastside Week* 5, no. 37 (May 5, 1995): 15–26.

"In Praise of the Tangled Bank." *Illahee* 10, no. 3 (Fall 1994): 178–80.

"The Local Connection." *Defenders* 69, no. 3 (Summer 1994): 33, 35.

"Prelude." *Journal of the Gurry Society* 1 (May 1994): 2.

"Documenting Our Place: The Art of Writing for Ourselves and the Land." *Pratt Museum Newsletter* 2, no. 2 (May 1994): 1.

"Damning the Sacred." *Illahee* 10, no. 4 (Winter 1994): 247–50.

"Receding from Grief." *Orion* 13, no. 1 (Winter 1994): 2–3.

"Magpie Days." *Petroglyph* 5 (1994): 18–23.

"The Meaning of Life." *Seattle Weekly* (December 15, 1993): 87.

"No Soil Required." *Left Bank* 5 (December 1993): 129–32.

"Magdalena Alpine: Black Glider of the Rockslides." *American Butterflies* 1, no. 4 (November 1993): 4–9.

"Plains Cottonwood." *American Horticulturalist* 72, no. 8 (August 1993): 39–42.

"Spring Butterflies in the Gorge." *Chinook Trek* 7 (May 1993): 2.

"A Ditch in Time." *Audubon* 95, no. 2 (March/April 1993): 42–43.

"Intimate Relations and the Extinction of Experience." *Left Bank* 2 (Summer 1992): 61–69.

"Highlights of the 1991 Butterfly Season." *Scarabogram* New Series, no. 140 (December 1991): 3–4.

"Joys of the Suburban Jungle." *East Side Week* (April 10, 1991).

"Housing Boom for Butterflies." *Wings* 15, no. 3 (Winter 1991): 3.

"A Vision for Future Forestry." *High Country News* 22, no. 22 (November 19, 1990): 29–30.

"Why Senescence (Rot) Is Not a Dirty Word." *High Country News* 22, no. 22 (November 19, 1990): 28.

"Willapa, Chopaka, and Inchelium: Recent Butterfly Activities." *Scarabogram* New Series, no. 125 (September 1990): 3–4.

"The Monarch Should Be Our National Insect." *Keystone Gardener* 49, no. 3 (Summer 1990): 21.

"Owls versus Timber: Is Compromise Possible? Future Demands Cooperation." *Chinook Observer* (June 13, 1990): 5–6.

"Logging Profits Control Forestry." *Wahkiakum County Eagle* (March 22, 1990).

"Spineless Wonders." *International Wildlife* 19, no. 5 (September/October 1989): 14–17.

"Monarch Butterflies: Messengers for Invertebrates." *Wings* 14, no. 2 (Summer 1989): 11.

"For the Love of Stumps." *Washington* 5, no. 6 (March/April 1989): 168–66.

"The Enchantments." *Oregonian Northwest Magazine* (October 16, 1988): 14–17.

"Close Encounters: A Naturalist Looks at the Ethics of 'First Contact.'" *Washington* 5, no. 2 (September/October 1988): 68–69.

Editorial on National Insect. *Northwest Lepidopterists' Association Newsletter* (April 15, 1988): 1.

"The Birth of Xerces." *Scarabogram* New Series, no. 91 (October 1987): 1–3.

"The Hills of Willapa." *Seattle Times Pacific Magazine* (March 15, 1987): 14–21.

"Monarch Should Be National Insect." *Wings* 12, no. 3 (Winter 1987): 2.

"The Joy of Butterflying." *Wings* 11, no. 3 (December 1984): 6–7.

"The Joy of Butterflying." *Audubon* 86, no. 4 (July/August 1984): 34–43.

"Spectacular!" *International Wildlife* 13, no. 6 (November/December 1983): 40–41.

"Migratory Monarchs: An Endangered Phenomenon." *Nature Conservancy News* 34, no. 5 (September/October 1983): 20–24.

"Oh, Those Urban Butterflies." *Urban Naturalist* (Summer 1983): 6–8.

"Gaining an Education as a Naturalist." *Orion Nature Quarterly* 1, no. 3 (Winter 1983): 32–35.

"The Niche of a Naturalist." *Orion Nature Quarterly* 1, no. 2 (Autumn 1982): 34–37.

"The Niche of a Naturalist." *Orion Nature Quarterly* 1, no. 1 (Summer 1982): 24–27.

"Many Butterflies Fluttering Near Edge of Extinction." *Chicago Tribune* (June 6, 1981): 9–10.

"Butterflies: Now You See Them . . ." *International Wildlife* 11, no. 1 (January/February 1981): 4–11.

"Loss of a Butterfly: Britain, *Maculinea arion*." *Wings* 6, no. 3 (December 11, 1979): 4–5.

"State Insects: The Oregon Swallowtail." *Wings* 6, no. 3 (December 11, 1979): 4–5.

"Particular Pleasures of Small Islands." *Pacific Search* 13, no. 11 (November 1979): 41–45.

"Big Worms." *Wings* 6, no. 1 (May 1979): 13.

"Butterflies Represented at World Conservation Meeting." *Wings* 6, no. 1 (May 1979): 4–5.

"How to Conserve Insects for Fun and Necessity." *Terra* 17, no. 4 (Spring 1979): 18–22.

"Natural Corral." *Nature Conservancy News* 29, no. 1 (January/February 1979): 20–21.

"A Xerces Society Office Fundraising Campaign, and Editorial." *Atala* 7, no. 1 (1979 (81)): 1.

"Comments on the Lepidopterists' Society Conservation Questionnaire." *Atala* 7, no. 1 (1979 (81)): 24–26.

"Wildlife and Warriors." *Horticulture* 56, no. 12 (December 1978): 32–36.

"Big Soos Butterfly Reserve Moves Toward Reality." *Wings* 5, no. 2 (November 20, 1978): 18.

"Xerces Society: A Brief History." *Wings* 5, no. 2
(November 20, 1978): 3.

"The Northwest Land Steward." *Oregon Chapter Newsletter*
(The Nature Conservancy) (Summer 1978): 7.

"Cascade Head." *Nature Conservancy News* 28, no. 2
(March/April 1978): 18–19.

"The Importance of Thinking Small." *Nature Conservancy
News* 28, no. 2 (March/April 1978): 25–26, 30.

"The Extinction of Experience." *Horticulture* 56, no. 1
(January 1978): 64–67.

"City Wildlife." *Horticulture* 55, no. 1 (January 1977):
65–69.

"Bans Alone Will Not Save Butterflies." *Sunday Times*
(London) (September 19, 1976): 15.

"The Bramble Patch Trap." *Horticulture* 54, no. 8 (August
1976): 14–17.

"Death of a Moth: Rejoinder to Virginia Woolf." *News of
the Lepidopterists' Society,* no. 1 (February 20, 1976): 1.

"The Lepidoptera Specialist Group Holds Its Inaugural
Meeting." *Atala* 4, nos. 1–2 (1976): 29.

"Presidential Message." *Atala* 4, nos. 1–2 (1976): 2–3.

"Symposium on Endangered Insects Held at 15th Congress
of Entomology, Washington, D.C., in August 1976."
Atala 4, nos. 1–2 (1976): 30.

"Create a Community Butterfly Reserve." *Xerces Society
Self-Help Sheet,* no. 4 (December 15, 1975): 1–4.

"Dams, an Editorial." *Atala* 3, no. 2 (Fall/Winter 1975): 37.

"The Butterflies of the National Parks." *National Parks and
Conservation* 49, no. 9 (September 1975): 10–14.

"Silk Moth of the Railroad Yards." *Natural History* 84, no. 5
(May 1975): 44–51.

"Interview with Paul Opler." *Atala* 3, no. 1 (Spring 1975):
2–3, 18–20.

"Tiger Beetles Endangered by Dune Buggies and Dams."
Atala 3, no. 1 (Spring 1975): 21.

"Our Friends, the Insects." *New York Times* (January 9,
1975): 34C.

"Is Brood 11 of the Periodical Cicada Extinct?" *Atala* 3, no. 1 (1975): 21.

"Proposed Policy on Insect Collecting." *Atala* 3, no. 1 (1975): 24.

"Railways and Butterflies." *Xerces Society Self-Help Sheet,* no. 2 (December 9, 1974): 1–8.

"Butterfly Watching and Conservation in Washington." *Seattle Audubon Notes* 14, no. 2 (October 1973): 4–6.

"Western Washington's Butterflies." *Seattle Times Magazine* (May 13, 1973): 4–5.

"Butterfly Watching in Washington, Part One: About Butterflies." *Seattle Audubon Notes* 13, no. 6 (February 1973): 6–7.

"A Colorado Yankee in Cromwell Country." *Cambridge-shire, Huntingdonshire, and Peterborough Life* 6, no. 65 (November 1972): 32–33.

"Christmas Bird Count, English Style, Part Two: The Red Hedge." *Seattle Audubon Notes* 12, no. 9 (May 1972): 6–7.

"Christmas Bird Count, English Style, Part One." *Seattle Audubon Notes* 12, no. 8 (April 1972): 4–5.

"Can We Save Our Wild Places? National Parks in Jeopardy." *American West* 9, no. 2 (March 1972): 36–41.

With John C. Hendee. "Wilderness Managers, Wilderness Users—A Problem of Perception." *Naturalist* 22, no. 3 (Autumn 1971): 22–26.

"Willapa Bay." *Audubon* 72, no. 6 (November/December 1970): 145.

"A Walk Around Campus." *University of Washington Daily Environmental Special Issue* (April 20, 1970): D4.

"Environmental Majors . . . What Route to Take?" *University of Washington Daily Environmental Special Issue* (April 20, 1970): D7.

"A Nature Walk Through Fort Lawton's Woodlands." *Pacific Search* 4, no. 7 (April 1970): 5.

"Newport High Symposium: Ecology Action." *Seattle Audubon Notes* 10, no. 7 (March 1970): 8.

"A Summer's Birding in Europe, Part Four." *Seattle Audubon Notes* 10, no. 6 (February 1970): 3.

"A Summer's Birding in Europe, Part Three." *Seattle Audubon Notes* 10, no. 5 (January 1970): 9–10.

"Is There Wilderness In Western Europe?" *Living Wilderness* 34, no. 112 (Winter 1970): 44–48.

"A Summer's Birding in Europe, Part Two." *Seattle Audubon Notes* 10, no. 4 (December 1969): 10.

"Union Bay Plant-In Statement." *Helix* 10, no. 7 (November 20, 1969): 2–3.

"A Summer's Birding in Europe, Part One." *Seattle Audubon Notes* 10, no. 2 (October 1969): 9.

"Four-Wheel Drive and the Outdoor Experience." *Northwest Conifer* 10, no. 2 (May 1969): 11–12.

"On Immensity and Usufruct." *Northwest Conifer* 9, no. 5 (December 1968): 9–11.

"Who Protects Endangered Butterflies?" *Defenders of Wildlife News* 43, no. 3 (July/August/September 1968): 295–98.

"A Case for Predators." *Seattle Times Charmed Land Magazine* (July 7, 1968): 10–11.

"Our Wilderness Anniversary." *Living Wilderness* 32, no. 102 (Summer 1968): 27–32.

"Point of Arches." *Northwest Conifer* 9, no. 3 (May 1968): 14.

"Butterflies for Birders." *Seattle Audubon Notes* 8, no. 9 (May 1968): 7.

"Conservation and Natural History." *Northwest Conifer* 9, no. 2 (March 1968): 11–12.

"Conservation: A Student Role." *Tyee* 3, no. 2 (Winter 1968): 24–32.

"Helen Lee Lemmon (1916–1967)." *Journal of the Lepidopterists' Society* 22, no. 3 (1968): 196.

"Statement on H.R. 8970, to Establish the North Cascades National Park." *The North Cascades*, Part I: Record of Hearings before the Subcommittee on National Parks and Recreation of the Committee on Interior and Insular Affairs, House of Representatives, Ninetieth Congress. Hearings held in Seattle, April 19–20, 1968. Washington, D.C.: Serial No. 90–24, U.S. Government Printing Office (1968): 201–202.

"Discover an Urban Sanctuary—Then Save It!" *Northwest Conifer* 8, no. 4 (September 1967): 7–8, 10.

"Help Sought to Keep High Line Canal Beautiful." *Aurora (Colo.) Advocate* (August 23, 1967): 17, 21.

"Camp Out." (Commentary on North Cascades hike-in with Justice William O. Douglas.) *University of Washington Daily* (Summer 1967).

"Cascades Panel." (Commentary on North Cascades conservation.) *University of Washington Daily* (Spring 1967).

"Statement on S. 1321, to establish the North Cascades National Park." *North Cascades*: Record of Hearings before the Subcommittee on Parks and Recreation of the Committee on Interior and Insular Affairs, United States Senate, Ninetieth Congress. Hearings held in Seattle, May 25, 1967. Washington: U.S. Government Printing Office (1967): 255–58.

"Don't Dam(n) It—Save It!" *Twang* 4, no. 4 (May 20, 1966): 1.

SCIENTIFIC PAPERS AND NOTES

With Lincoln P. Brower. "Mexican-American Interchange of Western Monarchs, and Their Floral Corridors." In *Migratory Pollinators and Their Corridors,* edited by Gary P. Nabhan. Tucson: University of Arizona Press, 2000.

With T. New, J. A. Thomas, C. D. Thomas, and P. C. Hammond. "Butterfly Conservation Management." *Annual Review of Entomology* 40 (1995): 57–83.

"A History of Lepidoptera Conservation, with Special Reference to Its Remingtonian Debt." *Journal of the Lepidopterists' Society* 49, no. 4 (1995): 397–411.

"An Ello Sphinx Moth Reared from an Ornamental Plant in Washington." *Northwest Lepidopterists' Association Newsletter* (Summer 1993): 3–4.

"Chinquapins and Hairstreaks." *Douglasia* 9, no. 1 (Winter 1990): 6.

"Washington Butterfly Conservation Status Report and Plan." Consultancy Report. Olympia: Department of Wildlife, 1989: 109 pp.

"Captive Breeding of Butterflies for Conservation." *Proceedings: Fifth World Conference on Breeding Endangered Species in Captivity*. Cincinnati: Cincinnati Zoo, Center for Reproduction of Endangered Wildlife, 1988.

"Investigation and Monitoring Report: Oregon Silverspot Butterfly in Pacific County, Washington." Consultancy Report. Olympia: U.S. Fish and Wildlife Service, Office of Endangered Species, 1985.

"The Impact of Recent Vulcanism on Lepidoptera." In *The Biology of Butterflies*, edited by R. L. Vane-Wright and P. H. Ackery, 323–26. London: Academic Press, 1984.

"Rebuttal to Murphy and Ehrlich on Common Names of Butterflies." *Journal of Research on the Lepidoptera* 23, no. 1 (1984): 89–93.

With M. G. Morris. In *Butterfly Farming in Papua New Guinea,* edited by Noel Vietmeyer, 1–34. Washington, D.C.: National Academy Press, 1983.

"Urbanization and Endangered Insect Populations." In *Urban Entomology: Interdisciplinary Perspectives*, edited by G. W. Frankie and C. S. Koehler, 376–94. New York: Prager, 1983.

With Michael Bentzien and Paul Opler. "Insect Conservation." *Annual Review of Entomology* 26 (1981): 233–58.

"International Efforts for Monarch Conservation, and Conclusion." *Atala* 9, nos. 1–2 (in English and Spanish) (1981 (84)): 21–22.

"Symposium on the Biology and Conservation of Monarch
  Butterflies." *Atala* 9, nos. 1–2 (in English and Spanish)
  (1981 (84)): 1.
"The Role of IUCN and WWF in Lepidoptera
  Conservation." In *Biotop- und Artenschutz bei
  Schmetterlingen*, edited by Günter Schmidt, 15–18.
  Karlsruhe, Germany: Institut für Okologie und
  Naturschutz, 1981.
With John Hinchliff, David V. McCorkle, Jonathan P.
  Pelham, and Jon H. Shepard. "A Check-List of
  Washington Butterflies." *Atala* 8, no. 1 (1980 (82)):
  27–29.
"Butterfly Eco-Geography and Biological Conservation in
  Washington." *Atala* 8, no. 1 (1980 (82)): 1–26.
"Common Names for North American Butterflies." *Atala* 8,
  no. 1 (1980 (82)): 31.
"Origins of the Washington Butterfly Fauna: Abstract."
  Abstracts of Submitted Papers, 26th Annual Meeting,
  Pacific Slope Section of the Lepidopterists' Society,
  University of California-Davis, August 24–26, 1979, 3–4.
"Editor's Note and Postscript to the British Issue." *Atala* 7,
  no. 2 (1979 (81)): 72.
"International Red Data Book of Invertebrates." *Atala* 7,
  no. 2 (1979 (81)): 60.
"Introduction to the British Issue." *Atala* 7, no. 2 (1979
  (81)): 33–34.
"Lepidoptera Conservation in Great Britain." *Atala* 7, no. 2
  (1979 (81)): 34–43.
"Recent IUCN Activity in Insect Conservation." *Atala* 7,
  no. 1 (1979 (81)): 26–27.
"International Problems in Insect Conservation." *Atala* 6,
  nos. 1–2 (1979 (81)): 56–58.
"IUCN and Insect Conservation." *Antenna* (London) 2,
  no. 2 (April 1978): 36.
"The Old Growth Forest in Wildlife Conservation."
  Abstracts, 59th Meeting, Pacific Division, American

Association for the Advancement of Science, June
13–17, 1978, 25.

With Sarah Anne Hughes. "Conservation and Utilization
of the Insect Resource of Papua New Guinea." Consultancy report to Wildlife Branch, Department of
Natural Resources, Port Moresby (1978): 1–157.

"The Eco-Geographic Basis for Lepidoptera Conservation."
Dissertation Abstracts International 37, no. 7 (1977):
3254-B–3255-B.

"Conservation of Lepidoptera in the United States."
Abstract 7E7223. *Entomology Abstracts* 7, no. 11
(November 1976): 122.

"The Scientific Management of Butterfly and Moth
Populations: A New Thrust of Wildlife Conservation."
Discovery 11, no. 2 (Spring 1976): 68–77.

"Conservation of Lepidoptera in the United States."
Biological Conservation 9, no. 1 (January 1976):
55–75.

"The Status of the Valerata Arctic." *Atala* 3, no. 2
(Fall/Winter 1975): 32–35.

"A Bibliography of Literature Related to Lepidoptera
Conservation." *Atala* 2, no. 1 (June 1974): 3–7.

"Boloria selene Ambushed by a True Bug." *Journal of the
Lepidopterists' Society* 27, no. 4 (1973): 305–307.

"The Heath Fritillary Survey." Abbots Ripton (U.K.): Nature
Conservancy, 1972: 1–7.

"Limenitis lorquini Attacking a Glaucous-winged Gull."
Journal of the Lepidopterists' Society 26, no. 4 (1972): 261.

"The Butterflies of the Highline Canal of Colorado: A First
Report." *Mid-Continent Lepidoptera Series* 2, no. 24
(February 1971): 1–19.

"Butterfly Protection: Sentiment *and* Sagacity." *Bulletin
of the Association of Minnesota Entomologists* 2, no. 4
(1968): 78–80.

"An Extraordinary Swarm of Butterflies in Colorado."
Journal of the Lepidopterists' Society 22, no. 3 (1968): 172.

"Conservation and the Lepidopterist." *Bulletin of the Association of Minnesota Entomologists* 2, no. 1 (September 1967): 1–5.

FICTION

"Nightlife with Insects." *Great Basin News* 1, no. 3 (Fall 1996): 14–18.
Excerpt from *Magdalena Mountain* (novel-in-progress). *American Butterflies* 1, no. 4 (November 1993): 10–12.
"Halloween Story." *Duckabush Journal* 1, no. 1 (Fall 1988): 7–9.

POEMS

"Evolution of the Genus *Iris*." *Isle* 7, no. 2 (Summer 2000).
"Lullaby for Pattiann." *Isle* 7, no. 2 (Summer 2000).
"Sheets on the Line." *Isle* 7, no. 2 (Summer 2000).
"Gulls at Rest." *Rain* (Spring 2000): 52.
"Coyote, Hit." *Wamka,* no. 5 (2000): 23.
"Silage." *Portland* 18, no. 4 (Winter 1999): 5.
"Out of Their Element." *Alaska Quarterly Review* 16, nos. 3–4 (Spring/Summer 1998): 168.
"Life and Death in Yellowstone." *Bear Essential* 9 (Winter 1997/1998): 19.
"Names of Things Here." *Portland* 16, no. 3 (Autumn 1997): 11.
"Pencil Shavings." *Rain* (Spring 1997): 2.
"Botany Lesson: Cleome." In *Crestone Chapbook*, edited by H. Parker Huber, 40. Brattleboro, Vt.: H. P. Huber, 1996.
"In July: Mock Orange." In *Syringa,* edited by Mary Clagett Smith, 17. Boise: Barbara Herrick, 1996.
"After Birth." *Convolvulus* 8 (Spring 1994): 4–5.
"Pseudotsuga menziesii." *Convolvulus* 8 (Spring 1994): 6.
"A Moon I Didn't See." In *Moon Museum,* edited by Patricia Staton Thomas. Seaview, Wash.: Heartbreak Prèss, 1992.

"Bonfire." *From the Lost Corner* 2, no. 2 (November 1, 1991): 9.

"Haiku Cycle from Bellingham." *Lynx* (Spring/Summer 1991): 7.

"Hearth." *From the Lost Corner* 2, no. 1 (May 1, 1991): 16.

"Birds, Out of Range." *Willapa Whistler* (March/April 1991): 6–7.

"Sequoias I Have Known." *From the Lost Corner* 1, no. 4 (February 1, 1991): 17.

"Wheatland Ferry." *From the Lost Corner* 1, no. 4 (February 1, 1991): 7.

"Crescent Lake: October 21, 1989." *From the Lost Corner* 1, no. 3 (November 1, 1990): 13–14.

"Spring Equinox (The Daffodils Came)." *From the Lost Corner* 1, no. 1 (May 1, 1990): 15.

"Aeschna." *Scarabogram* New Series, no. 120 (April 1990): 2–3.

"March." *Tapjoe* 6 (Spring 1990): 13–14.

"Purple Poesy." *Deception Pass Review* 1 (March 1989): 14.

"Hart's Pass, October 1, 1988." *Hart's Pass Review* 1 (October 1988): 2.

"Moon Walk." *Hart's Pass Review* 1 (October 1988): 1.

"Cat Report for Snohomish County." *Duckabush Journal* 1, no. 1 (Fall 1988): 6.

"Evolution" and "UV Reflection." In *The Alphabetical Coloring Book for Limerick-Loving Lepidopterists*, edited by Jo Brewer, 11, 41. Waltham, Mass: Capra Press, 1975.

BOOK INTRODUCTIONS

Intricate Homeland: Writings from the Klamath-Siskiyou, edited by Susan Cross. Ashland, Oreg.: Headwaters Press, 2000.

"Between Climb and Cloud: Nabokov Among the Lepidopterists." In *Nabokov's Butterflies*. Boston: Beacon Press, 2000.

"Reflections in a Golden Eye." In *Nature's Fading Chorus: Classic and Contemporary Writings on Amphibians,* edited by Gordon Miller. Washington, D.C.: Island Press, 2000.

"No Vacancy." In *Wild in the City*, edited by Michael Houck and M. J. Cody. Portland, Oreg.: Portland Audubon Society, 2000.

Not Just Trees: The Legacy of a Douglas-Fir Forest, by Jane Claire Dirks-Edmunds. Pullman: Washington State University Press, 1999.

Spirit of the Siskiyous: The Journals of a Mountain Naturalist, by Mary Paetzel. Corvallis: Oregon State University Press, 1999.

Wings for My Flight: The Peregrine Falcons of Chimney Rock, by Marcy Cottrell Houle. Boulder, Colo.: Pruett Publishing Company, 1999.

"John Heath: Insect Mapper and Conservationist Extraordinaire." In *Catalog of the Insect Conservation Literature Donated by Robert M. Pyle to the Systematic Entomology Laboratory, Department of Entomology, Oregon State University.* No. 1, by Gary L. Parsons, Anne Christie, and John D. Lattin. Corvallis: Arthropod Conservation Center, 1997.

South of Seattle, by James LeMonds. Missoula: Mountain Press, 1997.

Atlas of Washington Butterflies, by John Hinchliff. Corvallis: Oregon State University Bookstore, 1996.

Enduring Forests, edited by Ruth Kirk and Charles Mauzy. Seattle: Mountaineers, 1996.

Under Linden Trees (essay workshop anthology). Port Townsend: Centrum, 1991.

Art of the Butterfly, by Ed Marquand. San Francisco: Chronicle Books, 1990.

Butterfly Gardening: Creating Summer Magic in Your Garden, by the Xerces Society with the Smithsonian Institution. San Francisco: Sierra Club Books, 1990. Revised edition, San Francisco: Sierra Club Books, 1998.

The Butterfly Garden, by Mathew Tekulsky. Boston: Harvard
Common Press, 1985.

ANTHOLOGY APPEARANCES

"Eden in a Vacant Lot: Special Places, Species, and Kids in
the Community of Life." In *Children and Nature,* edited
by Stephen Kellert and Peter Kahn. Cambridge: MIT
Press, 2000.

"Field Notes." In *Getting Over the Color Green,* edited by
Scott Slovic. Tucson: University of Arizona Press, 2000.

"Waterproof Wildlife," an excerpt from *Wintergreen.* In
*Nature's Fading Chorus: Classic and Contemporary
Writings of Amphibians.* Washington, D.C.: Island Press,
2000.

"Bright Butterflies, Big City." In *Wild in the City*, edited
by Michael Houck and M. J. Cody. Portland, Oreg.:
Portland Audubon Society, 2000.

Excerpts from *The Thunder Tree.* In *Our Land, Ourselves:
Readings on People and Place*, edited by Peter Forbes, Ann
Armbrecht Forbes, and Helen Whybrow. San Francisco:
The Trust for Public Land, 1999.

"Butterflies: Conservation and Habitat." In *Conservation
and Environmentalism: An Encyclopedia*, edited by Robert
Paehlke. New York: Garland Publishing, 1995.

"Secrets of the Talking Leaf." In *Facing the Lion*, edited
by Kurt Brown. Boston: Beacon Press, 1995.

"A Grand Surprise," a chapter from *The Thunder Tree.* In
Words from The Land, edited by Stephen Trimble. Reno:
University of Nevada Press, 1995.

"A Flicker of Color by Night." In *The Cottage Book*, edited
by Frank B. Edwards. Newburg Lake, Ontario: Hedgehog
Productions, 1991.

"Butterfly Watching Tips." In *Butterfly Gardening: Creating
Summer Magic in Your Garden*, by the Xerces Society with
the Smithsonian Institution. San Francisco: Sierra Club

Books, 1990. Revised edition, San Francisco: Sierra Club
Books, 1998.

"And the Coyote Will Lift a Leg." In *The Norton Book of
Nature Writing,* edited by Robert Finch and John Elder.
New York: Norton, 1990.

"The Joy of Butterflying." In *Audubon Nature Yearbook,*
edited by Les Line. New York: Grolier, 1987.

Butterfly species accounts. In *Audubon Society Nature
Guides*, 7 vols. New York: Alfred A. Knopf, 1985.

"Management of Nature Reserves." In *Conservation Biology:
An Evolutionary-Ecological Perspective*, edited by Michael
Soule and Bruce Wilcox. Sunderland, Mass: Sinauer,
1980.

"Collections and Field Notes." In *Interpreting the
Environment*, edited by Grant W. Sharpe. New York:
Wiley, 1976. Revised edition, New York: Wiley, 1982.

"Extinct and Endangered Butterflies." In *Wildlife '76: The
World Conservation Yearbook*, edited by Nigel Sitwell.
London: Danbury Press, 1976.

"Union Bay: A Life-After-Death Plant-In." In *Ecotactics: The
Sierra Club Handbook for Environment Activists*, edited by
John G. Mitchell and Constance L. Stallings. New York:
Simon and Schuster, Pocket Books, 1970.

SOUND RECORDINGS

Interview by Steve Scher on KUOW Public Radio, Seattle,
January 6, 2000.

Reading of *Chasing Monarchs* recorded at Haystack Summer
Program in the Arts and Sciences, Cannon Beach, Oreg.,
aired on KMUN, Astoria, Oreg., November 1999.

"Animal Talk." Interview by Steve Paulson on *To the Best of
Our Knowledge*, Public Radio International, October 3,
1999.

Interview by Ginni Callihan on *The Writer's Block*, KMUN,
Astoria, Oreg., September 10, 1997.

"Nature and Childhood." Interview by Michael Silverblatt with Scott Russell Sanders on *Bookworm,* KCRW Public Radio, Los Angeles, Calif., April 17, 1996.

Interview by Vicki Gaberaux, Canadian Broadcasting Company, Vancouver, British Colombia, October 27, 1995.

Recorded plenary lecture, Fourth Annual Watchable Wildlife Conference, Estes Park, Colo., September 20, 1995.

Interview by Morgan Holm on *Oregon Considered*, KOAP, Portland, Oreg., August 15, 1995.

Interview by Nick Forster on *E-Town*, National Public Radio, August 1995.

"Going to Sturgis?" A short story read by Nancy Montgomery on *A Story Told,* KMUN, Astoria, Oreg., May 28, 1995.

Reading of *Where Bigfoot Walks*, a recording of "Secret Places," Orion Society Forgotten Language Tour, University of Arizona, Tempe, Ariz., April 4, 1995.

Interview by Steve Scher on *Seattle Afternoon*, KUOW Public Radio, Seattle, August 1995.

Interview on *The Weirdo Hour,* KOA, Denver, August 1995.

"Like Water for Coffee." A short story read by Nancy Montgomery on *A Story Told,* KMUN, Astoria, Oreg., December 27, 1994.

"Slug Love and Spider Hate." An essay from *Wintergreen* read by Sylvia Berkman on *Late Night Erotica*, KMUN, Astoria, Oreg., 1989.

VIDEO RECORDINGS

Reading of *Chasing Monarchs*, Pacific Grove Museum of Natural History, Pacific Grove, California, October 1999.

Interview. *Bigfoot: Discovery of World Mysteries*. Robin Tani/Media Factory, Tokyo, Japan, August 16, 1999.

Sasquatch Odyssey: The Hunt for Bigfoot. Big Hairy Deal
Films, Inc., Vancouver, British Colombia, August 30,
1998.

Interview. *Good Morning America,* ABC, June 1998.

INTERVIEWS

Baker, Jeff. "Tracking Bigfoot, Step by Giant Step." *Sunday
Oregonian* (October 3, 1999).

Busse, Ruth Allington. "Robert Michael Pyle." In *Echoes of
the Valley: Oral Histories of Gray's River,* edited and published by Ruth Allington Busse. Seattle, 2000.

Cassell, Faris. "Hearts All Aflutter." *Eugene Register-Guard*
(October 24, 1999).

Jackson, Peter. "Butterfly Man on Importance of
Invertebrates: Dr. Robert Pyle." *WWF Monthly Report*
(September 1980).

Jackson, Tom. "Chronicles of the Outdoors: Conservation
Author Practices What He Pens." *Panache!* (March 3,
1989).

Juillerat, Lee. "From Sea Shells to Butterflies." *Klamath Falls
(Oreg.) Herald & News* (October 7, 1999).

Kelleher, Ray. "From a Distance, the Study of Butterflies
Looks Like an Obsessive Pursuit of Nothing at All. On a
Figurative Level, the Same Could Be Said of the Writing
Life. An Interview with Robert Michael Pyle." *Poets &
Writers* 24, no. 2 (March/April 1996).

Lundegaard, Erik. "Chasing Butterflies." *Seattle Times*
(August 31, 1999).

McNamee, Gregory. "On the Wings of a Monarch: A
Conversation with Robert Michael Pyle." *Amazon.com*
(Autumn 1999).

Mosedale, Susan Sleeth. "An Imperiled Monarchy."
Northwest Magazine (November 18, 1984).

Pintarich, Paul. "Scientist-Author Blends Fiction, Nature in
Writing." *Oregonian* (January 20, 1987).

Rushing, Kathy. "Butterfly Man." *Audubon Naturalist* (April 1994).

Schmader, David. "Bio: Readings—Robert Michael Pyle." *The Stranger* (December 30–January 5, 2000).

Stepankowsky, Andrè. "Metamorphosis of a Naturalist." *Washington* 4, no. 1 (August 1987).

———. "Gray's River Biologist Fighting to Save Butterflies." *Longview (Wash.) Daily News* (June 11, 1984).

Stoenner, Herb. "Butterfly Watching 'Art Form.'" *Denver Post* (July 20, 1977).

Thorness, Bill. "Butterfly Fascination Leads to Career for Naturalist Granger." *Grange News* (February 1987).

Walker, Casey. "Interview with Robert Michael Pyle." *Wild Duck Review* 3, no. 1 (February 1997).

Williams, Terry Tempest. "Birdwatcher Discovers Wonder of Butterflies." *Deseret News* (August 5, 1984).

Wulff, Jane Elder. "Dr. Robert Michael Pyle: A Meticulous Observer of Life." *Peninsula* 7, no. 3 (Fall 1992).

BIOGRAPHICAL/CRITICAL STUDIES AND BOOK REVIEWS

Abbot, Deborah. Review of *A Field Guide to the Butterflies Coloring Book*. *Seattle Times* (November 13, 1983).

Adams, Phoebe-Lou. Review of *Where Bigfoot Walks*. *Atlantic Monthly* 276, no. 2 (August 1995).

Adlerstein, Laurie. Review of *Nabokov's Butterflies*. *New York Times Book Review* (May 7, 2000).

Aiello, Annette. Review of *The Audubon Society Handbook for Butterfly Watchers*. *Library Journal* 109, no. 11 (June 15, 1984).

Anderson, Ross. "Forever Green." Review of *Wintergreen*. *Seattle Times Pacific Magazine* (March 15, 1987).

Axness, Nancy and Willard. Review of *Wintergreen*. *H. Berry's Journal* 1, no. 1 (October 1988).

Baker, Jeff. "Bigfoot Search Yields Delightful Book." Review of *Where Bigfoot Walks. Sunday Oregonian* (July 23, 1995).

Banville, John. "Vlad the Impaler." Review of *Nabokov's Butterflies. Irish Times* (April 15, 2000).

Bate, Jonathan. "Lepidoptera and Lolita." Review of *Nabokov's Butterflies. Sunday Telegraph* (London) (March 19, 2000).

Baumgarten, Fred. Review of *Chasing Monarchs. Amicus Journal* 21, no. 4 (Winter 2000).

Becker, Alida. Review of *Wintergreen. Philadelphia Inquirer* (February 7, 1988).

Beifuss, John. "Biologist Preaches Respect for Bigfoot." Review of *Where Bigfoot Walks. Memphis Commercial Appeal* (September 10, 1995).

Borkin, Susan Sullivan. Review of *The Audubon Society Handbook for Butterfly Watchers. Lore* (Milwaukee Public Museum) 36, no. 2 (Summer 1986).

Brandt, Anthony. "Quests." Review of *Where Bigfoot Walks. Men's Journal* (September 1995).

Brown, Bruce. "Backwater Treading: Essayist in the Willapa Wilds Writes of Wonder and Dismay." *Seattle Times* (February 15, 1987).

Brown, Clarence. "A Passion for Butterflies, Lolita." Review of *Nabokov's Butterflies. Seattle Times* (April 28, 2000).

Buchholtz, C. W. "Ode to Highline Canal Sure to Please Local Readers." Review of *The Thunder Tree. Rocky Mountain News* (November 14, 1993).

———. "Legend of 'Bigfoot' Very Much Alive in Dying Wilderness." *Rocky Mountain News* (January 6, 1996).

Buckelew, Albert R., Jr. Review of *Handbook for Butterfly Watchers. Redstart* (July 1993).

Bunnelle, Hasse Russell. Review of *The Thunder Tree. Outdoors West* 16, no. 2 (Winter 1993/1994).

Camuto, Christopher. Review of *Chasing Monarchs. Audubon* 102, no. 2 (March/April 2000).

————. Review of *Wintergreen*. *Sierra* 72, no. 3 (May/June 1987).

Cannard, Don. Review of *The Thunder Tree*. *Chinook Trek*, no. 8 (August 1993).

Caras, Roger. Review of *The Audubon Society Handbook for Butterfly Watchers*. *Newsday* (July 31, 1984).

Carrier, Jim. "Last One in the High Line's a Grownup." *Denver Post* (May 5, 1993).

Chandonnet, Ann. Review of *The Thunder Tree*. *Writer's NW* (Winter 1993).

Chappell, Janet. "Maritime Lifestyles a Joy to Read." Review of *Wintergreen*. *Oregon Coast* (April/May 1987).

Clark, Jayne. Review of *Chasing Monarchs*. *USA Today* (September 10, 1999).

Cohen, James A. Review of *The Audubon Field Guide to North American Butterflies*. *Smithsonian* 12, no. 1 (February 1982).

Connelly, Joel. "Recycled Books, Classics Sprout for Earth Day." Review of *Wintergreen*. *Seattle Post-Intelligencer* (April 19, 1990).

Connor, Steve. "Nabokov: From Lepidopterology to 'Lolita.'" Review of *Nabokov's Butterflies*. *Independent* (London) (March 30, 2000).

Cowan, Ron. "Book Sings of Man and Nature." Review of *Wintergreen*. *Salem (Oreg.) Statesman-Journal* (February 10, 1988).

Cox, James A. Review of *Where Bigfoot Walks*. *Midwest Book Review* (Summer 1995).

Craig, Paul. "Nature Next-Door: Robert Michael Pyle's Suburban Boyhood Taught Him That Nature Can Be Found Even in Vacant Lots." *Spokane Spokesman-Review* (May 23, 1993).

Crawford, Rod. Review of *Wintergreen*. *Scarabogram* New Series, no. 83 (February 1987).

Dallas, Sandra. "Highline Canal Flows into Book." *Denver Post* (September 19, 1993).

Davis, Don. "The Minds of Bigfoot's Faithful: Author Explores This Murky Place." Review of *Where Bigfoot Walks*. *Walla Walla Union Bulletin* (August 16, 1995).

Devlin, Sherry. "Butterfly Believer." *Missoulian* (July 17, 1999).

Dixon, Terrell. "Inculcating Wildness: Rick Bass, Robert Michael Pyle, John Hanson Mitchell, and Teaching Urban Nature." *The Nature of Cities,* edited by Michael Bennett and David Teague. Tucson: University of Arizona Press, 1999.

Dominick, Richard B. Review of *Watching Washington Butterflies*. *Journal of the Lepidopterists' Society* 29, no. 1 (1975).

Doyle, Brian. "Naturalist Traces the Monarch Butterfly's Incredible Journeys." Review of *Chasing Monarchs. San Francisco Sunday Examiner and Chronicle* (September 19, 1999).

Drabelle, Dennis. "Desperately Seeking Sasquatch." Review of *Where Bigfoot Walks. Washington Post Book World* (July 16, 1995).

Dubail, Jean. "Natural Science, a Bit of Poetry." Review of *Chasing Monarchs. Cleveland Plain Dealer* (August 22, 1999).

Dunn, Gary A. Review of *Insects: A Peterson Field Guide Coloring Book. Young Entomologists' Society Quarterly* 11, no. 2 (April/June 1994).

Duthie, Niall. "Nabokov on the Wing." Review of *Nabokov's Butterflies. Scotsman* (March 18, 2000).

Earley, George W. "From Butterflies to Bigfoot." Review of *Where Bigfoot Walks. Upper Left Edge* (November 1995).

———. "Following in Rather Big Footsteps." Review of *Where Bigfoot Walks. Sunday Oregonian* (July 23, 1995).

Eckhoff, Sally. "The Monarch King Takes Flight." Review of *Chasing Monarchs. Newsday* (August 11, 1999).

Edgar, Blake. "In Hot Pursuit." Review of *Chasing Monarchs. California Wild* (Spring 2000).

Ehrlich, Paul R. and Dennis D. Murphy. Review of *The Audubon Society Handbook for Butterfly Watchers. Journal of Research on the Lepidoptera* 24, no. 4 (Winter 1985 (86)).

Ehrlich, Paul R. Review of *IUCN Invertebrate Red Data Book. Natural History* 92, no. 10 (October 1983).

English, Susan. "'Monarchs' Takes You on a Drive Through Western Terrain." Review of *Chasing Monarchs. Spokane Spokesman-Review* (October 17, 1999).

Ferris, Clifford D. Review of *The Audubon Society Field Guide to North American Butterflies. Journal of the Lepidopterists' Society* 37, no. 2 (1983).

Ford, Pat. "Rambles in a Ravaged Land." Review of *Wintergreen. High Country News* (November 19, 1990).

Fowles, John. "The High Ridges of Knowledge." Review of *Nabokov's Butterflies. Spectator* 284, no. 8958 (April 15, 2000).

Gall, Lawrence K. Review of *The Audubon Society Handbook for Butterfly Watchers. American Scientist* 74, no. 2 (March/April 1986).

Gee, Maggie. "Lepping Around on the Hilltops." Review of *Nabokov's Butterflies. Daily Telegraph* (London) (March 25, 2000).

Glotfelty, Cheryll. Review of *Wintergreen* and *The Thunder Tree. Western American Literature* 30, no. 3 (November 1995).

Gravelle, Judy. "Nature Book Is Joy to Read." Review of *Wintergreen. Duluth News-Tribune* (September 4, 1988).

Gudmundsen, Marilyn. Review of *A Field Guide to Butterflies Coloring Book. Wahkiakum County Eagle* (October 6, 1983).

Harvey, Miles. "Dances with Bigfoot." Review of *Where Bigfoot Walks. Outside* 20, no. 8 (August 1995).

Hay, John. "On *Wintergreen*." Review of *Wintergreen. Wake-Robin* 21, no. 3 (February 1987).

Heffernan, Maureen. Review of *The Thunder Tree. American Horticulturist* 72, no. 8 (August 1993).

Heilenman, Diane. "Butterflies May Not Be Free, but They're Cheap." Review of *Handbook for Butterfly Watchers*. *Louisville (Ky.) Courier-Journal* (June 18, 1992).

Heilman, Robert. Review of *The Thunder Tree*. *Seattle Weekly* (October 13, 1993).

Hodgson, Dick. Review of *The Thunder Tree*. *Trail and Timberline* (Colorado Mountain Club), no. 888 (November 1993).

Holt, John. "A Good Ditch, and Feathery Tales." Review of *The Thunder Tree*. *Kinesis* 2, no. 8 (August 1993).

Hornaday, James C. "Documenting Our Place: The Art of Writing for Ourselves and the Land." *Homer Tribune* (May 10, 1994).

Howard, Toby. "Down in the Woods, Something Stirs." Review of *Where Bigfoot Walks*. *New Scientist* 147, no. 1989 (August 5, 1995).

Howell, Bill. Review of *Chasing Monarchs*. *Monarch News* 9, no. 9 (June 1999).

Hugo, Nancy. "Butterfly Watching." Review of *Handbook for Butterfly Watchers*. *Virginia Wildlife* (July 1996).

Hunt, Bill. Review of *Where Bigfoot Walks*. *Anchorage Daily News* (October 1, 1995).

Hunt, Ed. "Area Writer Tracks Legend of Bigfoot." *Chinook Observer* and *Panache!* Review of *Where Bigfoot Walks*. (July 28, 1995).

Kakutani, Michiko. "How Chasing Butterflies Can Become a Marathon." Review of *Chasing Monarchs*. *New York Times* (August 13, 1999). Reprinted as "Fascination and Knowledge Drive Writer's Tracking of Monarchs." *Seattle Post-Intelligencer* (August 20, 1999). Reprinted as "Monarchs are the Kings of Travelers?" *Omaha World-Herald* (August 22, 1999).

Karges, Joann. "Beauty to Enjoy, Protect." *Fort Worth Star-Telegram* (November 11, 1984).

———. Review of *Wintergreen*. *News of the Fort Worth Nature Center and Refuge* (March 1988).

Kellerman, Stewart. "Nothing But Net." Review of *Chasing Monarchs*. *New York Times Book Review* (August 15, 1999). Reprinted in *Scarabogram* New Series, no. 232 (August 1999).

Kenney, Michael. "'Monarch' Soars with Fine Writing, Colorful Observation." Review of *Chasing Monarchs*. *Boston Globe* (August 23, 1999). Reprinted as "Soaring with the Monarchs." *Detroit News* (September 25, 1999) and as "Flights of Fancy." *San Jose Mercury News* (September 12, 1999).

Kimura, Michio and Dan Carney. Review of *Watching Washington Butterflies*. *Pacific Search* 9, no. 1 (October 1974).

Kisling, Jack. Review of *Wintergreen*. *Denver Post* (March 13, 1988).

Kruckeberg, Arthur. Review of *Chasing Monarchs*. *Douglasia* 24, no. 1 (Winter 2000).

———. "Nature Bats Last in Willapa Hills." Review of *Wintergreen*. *Douglasia* 12, no. 1 (Winter 1988).

Kuhlken, Robert. "Robert Michael Pyle: A Critical Assessment." http://www.cwu.edu/-geography/pyle.html, Central Washington University, 2000.

LeMonds, James. "From Butterflies to Bigfoot." Review of *Where Bigfoot Walks*. *English Journal* 85, no. 6 (October 1996).

———. Review of *The Thunder Tree*. *English Journal* 83, no. 7 (November 1994).

Lichtenberg, Carol J. Review of *Wintergreen*. *Library Journal* 112, no. 2 (February 1, 1987).

Little, Charles E. "Books for the Wilderness." Review of *Wintergreen*. *Wilderness* 51, no. 181 (Summer 1988).

Lopez, Michael. "Migration of the Monarch." Review of *Chasing Monarchs*. *Albany Times Union* (October 19, 1999).

Loshbaugh, Shana. "Workshop Paints Nature-Writer's Vista." *Homer News* (May 5, 1994).

L.R. Review of *A Field Guide to the Butterflies Coloring Book*. *Seattle Times* (November 13, 1983) and *Seattle Post-Intelligencer* (November 29, 1983).

Lukas, David. Review of *Chasing Monarchs*. *Orion* 19, no. 2 (Spring 2000).

Manion, Christian. "*Chasing Monarchs*: Another Perspective." Review of *Chasing Monarchs*. *Monarch News* 9, no. 10 (July 1999).

Marshall, John. "A Naturalist Hunts Bigfoot." Review of *Where Bigfoot Walks*. *Seattle Post-Intelligencer* and *Sarasota Herald-Tribune* (August 20, 1995).

Marsi, Rick. "Three Spell-Binding Must Books for Butterfly Buffs." Review of *Handbook for Butterfly Watchers*. *Binghamton (N.Y.) Press & Sun-Bulletin* (August 15, 1993). Reprinted as "Three Butterfly Books Help Nature on the Fly." *Rochester (N.Y.) Democrat & Chronicle* (August 22, 1993).

Mars-Jones, Adam. "Forget Lolita . . . Let's Hear It For Lepidoptery. . . ." *Observer* (London) (March 19, 2000).

McDaniel, Lisa R. "Pull Up a Chair; Hear the Tales." Review of "Wheatland Ferry," a poem published in *From the Lost Corner* 1, no. 4 (1991). *Chinook Observer* (March 20, 1991).

McMichael, Barbara Lloyd. "One Man's Butterfly Quest Fascinating Journey." Review of *Chasing Monarchs*. *Bremerton (Wash.) Sun* (September 17, 1999). Reprinted as "Butterfly Travelogue as Charming as It Is Informative." *Olympian* (September 19, 1999); and as "In Search of Butterflies, New Vocabulary." *Tacoma News Tribune* (September 19, 1999).

McNulty, Tim. "Bigfoot's Turf." Review of *Where Bigfoot Walks*. *Seattle Times* (August 27, 1995).

———. "Save Nature: Farms Don't Sprout Malls." Review of *The Thunder Tree*. *Seattle Times* (August 1, 1993).

Meeuse, B. J. D. Review of *Watching Washington Butterflies*.

University of Washington Arboretum Bulletin 37, no. 4 (Fall 1974).

Montgomery, Sy. "King's Highway." Review of *Chasing Monarchs. Boston Globe* (September 6, 1999).

Moore, Kathleen Dean. "Pilgrimage with the Migrating Monarch." Review of *Chasing Monarchs. Sunday Oregonian* (September 26, 1999).

Morgan, Murray. "Writer Treks Psyche 'Looking Into Bigfoot.'" Review of *Where Bigfoot Walks. Tacoma News Tribune* (August 13, 1995).

Murray, Bill. "Highline Story Rich Experience." *Aurora (Colo.) Sentinel* (1994).

Nelson, Rick. "Gray's River Writer Hits the Mark with Book about Bigfoot." Review of *Where Bigfoot Walks. Wahkiakum (Wash.) County Eagle* (August 31, 1995).

———. "Gray's River Writer's New Book Highlights Interest." Review of *The Thunder Tree. Wahkiakum (Wash.) County Eagle* (June 3, 1993).

———. "Gray's River Writer Offers New Views of These Hills." Review of *Wintergreen. Wahkiakum (Wash.) County Eagle* (November 27, 1986).

Nichols, Kathryn McKenzie. "'Tracking the Monarchs' 'Sky River.'" Review of *Chasing Monarchs. Monterey County Herald* (October 8, 1999).

O'Connell, Thomas E. Review of *Chasing Monarchs. Earthcare Northwest* (Seattle Audubon Society) 41, no. 4 (December 1999/January 2000).

Orans, Muriel. Review of *A Field Guide to the Butterflies Coloring Book. Benton Bulletin* (December 21, 1983).

Orsak, Larry. "Appreciating Insects through Butterflies." Review of *Audubon Society Handbook for Butterfly Watchers. Bulletin of the Entomological Society of America* (Winter 1986).

Ortman, David. Review of *Wintergreen. Not Man Apart* 17, no. 2 (March/April 1987).

Osment, Noel. Review of *Wintergreen*. *San Diego Union* (February 7, 1988).

Parini, Jay. "The Wings of Desire." Review of *Nabokov's Butterflies*. *Guardian, Saturday Review* (March 25, 2000).

Parr, Barry. Review of *Chasing Monarchs*. *America West* (July 1999).

Patterson, Marion. Review of *Insects: A Peterson Field Guide Coloring Book*. *Cedar Rapids Gazette* (November 7, 1993).

Paulu, Tom. "Chasing Monarchs." *Longview (Wash.) Daily News* (September 3, 1999).

————. "Bigfoot Walks: Robert Pyle's New Book Explores Facts and Myths in the Dark Divide Area." Review of *Where Bigfoot Walks*. *Longview (Wash.) Daily News* (July 21, 1995).

Pepin, Yvonne. Review of *Wintergreen*. *Port Townsend Leader* (February 10, 1988).

Perez, Danny. Review of *Where Bigfoot Walks*. *Fate* 24, no. 1 (June 1996).

Peterson, Barbara C. Review of *The Thunder Tree: Lessons from an Urban Wildland*. *Northwest Environmental Journal* 9, nos. 1–2 (Fall/Winter 1993).

Peterson, David. Review of *Where Bigfoot Walks*. *Western American Literature* 30, no. 3 (November 1995).

Pierce, J. Kingston. Review of *Where Bigfoot Walks*. *Seattle* (July 1995).

Pierson, Michael. "Robert Michael Pyle." *American Nature Writers,* edited by John Elder. New York: Scribner, 1996.

Pintarich, Paul. "The Ravaging of the Green." Review of *Wintergreen*. *Oregonian Northwest Magazine* (January 4, 1987).

Ratliff, Ronald Ray. Review of *Nabokov's Butterflies*. *Library Journal* 125, no. 4 (March 1, 2000).

Reber, Jack. Review of *Wintergreen*. *San Diego Tribune* (February 27, 1987).

Review of *Nabokov's Butterflies*. *Scientific American* (June 2000).

Review of *Nabokov's Butterflies. Good Book Guide* (www.good-book-guide.com) (Spring 2000).

Review of *Nabokov's Butterflies. Publishers Weekly* 247, no. 11 (March 13, 2000).

Review of *Chasing Monarchs. Dallas Morning News* (January 30, 2000).

Review of *Chasing Monarchs. Current Books on Gardening and Botany* 1, no. 4 (December 1999).

Review of *Chasing Monarchs. Science News* 156, no. 8 (August 21, 1999).

Review of *Chasing Monarchs. Wahkiakum (Wash.) County Eagle* (August 19, 1999).

Review of *Chasing Monarchs. Kirkus Reviews* (June 15, 1999).

Review of *Chasing Monarchs. Publishers Weekly* 246, no. 23 (June 7, 1999).

Review of *Where Bigfoot Walks. Audubon Warbler* (Portland Audubon Society) 59, no. 11 (November 1995).

Review of *Where Bigfoot Walks. American Heritage* 46, no. 5 (September 1995).

Review of *Where Bigfoot Walks. Madison (Wis.) Capital Times* (August 18, 1995).

Review of *Where Bigfoot Walks. Publishers Weekly* 242, no. 24 (June 12, 1995).

Review of *Where Bigfoot Walks. Kirkus Reviews* (May 15, 1995).

Review of *The Thunder Tree. Journal of Forestry* 91, no. 12 (December 1993).

Review of *The Thunder Tree. Bookwatch* (July 1993).

Review of *The Thunder Tree. Wings* 17, no. 2 (Summer 1993).

Review of *The Thunder Tree. Publishers Weekly* 240, no. 11 (March 15, 1993).

Review of *Handbook for Butterfly Watchers. Pacific Horticulture* 53, no. 4 (Winter 1992).

Review of *Wintergreen. Pacific Horticulture* 53, no. 4 (Winter 1992).

Review of *Wintergreen*. *Sci-Tech Book News* (March 1987).

Review of *Wintergreen*. *Chattanooga Times* (February 11, 1987).

Review of *Wintergreen*. *Medford Mail Tribune* (January 30, 1987).

Review of *Wintergreen*. *Booklist* 83, no. 10 (January 15, 1987).

Review of *Wintergreen*. *Publishers Weekly* 230, no. 21 (November 21, 1986).

Review of *Wintergreen*. *Kirkus Reviews* (November 1, 1986).

Review of *The Audubon Society Handbook for Butterfly Watchers*. *American West* 21, no. 6 (November/December 1984).

Review of *The Audubon Society Handbook for Butterfly Watchers*. *Omaha Morning World-Herald* (September 23, 1984).

Review of *The Audubon Society Handbook for Butterfly Watchers*. *Science News* 126, no. 4 (July 28, 1984).

Review of *A Field Guide to the Butterflies Coloring Book*. *Science News* (December 10, 1983).

Review of *IUCN Invertebrate Red Data Book*. *San Luis Obispo Telegram-Tribune* (November 24, 1983).

Review of *The Audubon Field Guide to North American Butterflies*. *Booklist* 78, no. 4 (October 15, 1981).

Review of *The Audubon Field Guide to North American Butterflies*. *Los Angeles Times Book Review* (September 20, 1981).

Review of *The Audubon Field Guide to North American Butterflies*. Copley News Service (September 1981).

Review of *The Audubon Field Guide to North American Butterflies*. *Tulsa World* (August 9, 1981).

Rogers, Michael. Review of *Wintergreen*. *Library Journal* 121, no. 10 (June 1, 1996).

Ruprecht, Archie. "Your Outback and Mine." Review of *The Thunder Tree*. *Earth Letter* (November 1993).

Ryan, Kay. "Big Shoes to Fill." Review of *Where Bigfoot Walks*. *Hungry Mind Review* (Winter 1995/1996).

Samstag, Tony. "Putting Backbone Into Conservation." Review of *IUCN Invertebrate Red Data Book*. *Times* (London) (May 19, 1983).

Sandiford, Sheila. Review of *Wintergreen*. *Peninsula* 3, no. 4 (Winter 1988).

Sapp, Gregg. "Science at the Millennium: Best Sci-Tech Books 1999." Review of *Chasing Monarchs*. *Library Journal* (March 1, 2000).

———. Review of *Chasing Monarchs*. *Library Journal* 124, no. 12 (July 1999).

Satterwhite, Bob. "New Books Detail Fascinating World of Butterflies." *Asheville (N.C.) Citizen-Times* (May 31, 1992).

Scigliano, Eric. "Love Among the Stumps." Review of *Wintergreen*. *Seattle Weekly* (January 14–20, 1987).

———. "The Browser." Review of journal *Illahee*. *Seattle Weekly* (November 27, 1996).

Scott, James A. "Story of Forest Rambles." *Rocky Mountain News* (January 18, 1987).

———. Review of *The Audubon Field Guide to North American Butterflies*. *Journal of Research on the Lepidoptera* 20, no. 1 (1981 (82)).

Seaman, Donna. Review of *Nabokov's Butterflies*. *Booklist* 96, no. 14 (March 15, 2000).

———. Review of *Chasing Monarchs*. *Booklist* 95, no. 21 (July 1999).

Sexton, David. "A Genius Who Spreads His Wings." Review of *Nabokov's Butterflies*. *Sunday Herald* (Glasgow, Scotland) (March 26, 2000).

———. "The True Loves of Nabokov." Review of *Nabokov's Butterflies*. *Evening Standard* (London) (March 20, 2000).

Shalaway, Scott. Review of *Chasing Monarchs*. *Pittsburgh Post-Gazette* (November 28, 1999).

Shapiro, Arthur M. Review of *Watching Washington Butterflies*. *Journal of the Lepidopterists' Society* 29, no. 1 (1975).

Shields, Oakley. Review of *The Audubon Field Guide to North American Butterflies. Journal of Research on the Lepidoptera* 20, no. 1 (1981 (82)).

Shores, Elizabeth F. "Reconstructing Pivotal Times That Changed a Life." Review of *The Thunder Tree. Arkansas Democrat-Gazette* (November 21, 1993).

Silberglied, Robert E. Review of *The Audubon Field Guide to North American Butterflies. Library Journal* 106, no. 15 (September 15, 1981).

Smith, L. Review of *The Thunder Tree. Choice* 31, no. 2 (October 1993).

Stepankowsky, Andrè. "In Praise of Open Space: Pyle's New Book Is Love Song to Forgotten Lands." Review of *The Thunder Tree. Longview (Wash.) Daily News* (April 17, 1993).

———. "Willapa Mosaic Drawn with Loving Hand." Review of *Wintergreen. Longview (Wash.) Daily News* (January 31, 1987).

Sterba, James P. "Before You Squash That Bug, Be Sure It Isn't One We Need." Review of *IUCN Invertebrate Red Data Book. Wall Street Journal* (October 5, 1983).

Stiehm, Jamie. "Pyle's 'Chasing Monarchs': Tiny, Lovely, Mysterious." *Baltimore Sun* (August 15, 1999).

Stiles, Marc. "Beauty Found in Beaten Willapa Hills." Review of *Wintergreen. Chinook Observer* (December 3, 1986).

Stuttaford, Genevieve. Review of *Wintergreen. Publishers Weekly* 233, no. 47 (November 21, 1986).

Sullivan, Robert. "Sasquatchology: He's Huge, Hairy, Elusive, and Mythologically Necessary." Review of *Where Bigfoot Walks. New York Times Books Review* (July 30, 1995).

Sullivan, Roger. "Bigfoot Tale Walks Into Bookstores." Review of *Where Bigfoot Walks. Vancouver (Wash.) Columbian* (July 13, 1995).

Sumner-Mack, Nan. "Poetic Eye Turns Butterfly Study

Into an Insightful Gem." Review of *Chasing Monarchs*. *Providence Sunday Journal* (October 17, 1999).

Taylor, Robert. "Scientist, Artist Converge in *Nabokov's Butterflies*." Review of *Nabokov's Butterflies*. *Boston Globe* (May 3, 2000).

Thompson, Jeff and Lesley Norman. *"Wintergreen* Is about Local Area." *Comet's Tale* 3, no. 4 (January 30, 1987).

Travis, Wayne. Review of *Where Bigfoot Walks*. *Saratoga Springs (N.Y.) Saratogian* (August 13, 1995).

Trimnell, Angus. Review of *The Thunder Tree*. *Booklist* 89, no. 17 (May 1, 1993).

Tweit, Susan J. "Making the Leap from Science to Poetry: The Writing of Robert Michael Pyle." *Bloomsbury Review* 14, no. 4 (July/August 1994).

Varty, Alexander. Review of *Where Bigfoot Walks*. *Georgia Straight* (Vancouver, British Colombia) (November 23–30, 1995).

Vaughan, Valerie. Review of *Where Bigfoot Walks*. *Library Journal* 120, no. 12 (July 1995).

Walden, George. Review of *Nabokov's Butterflies*. *Literary Review* (March 2000).

Warshall, Peter. Review of *The Audubon Society Handbook for Butterfly Watchers*. *Whole Earth Review* (July 1985).

———. "Saving the Creepy Crawlies." Review of *IUCN Invertebrate Red Data Book*. *San Francisco Chronicle* (December 28, 1983).

Watson, Chris. "The Importance of Bigfoot." Review of *Where Bigfoot Walks*. *Santa Cruz County Sentinel* (July 21–27, 1995).

Watts, Alice. "Author Slides to Defense of Region's Creepy Crawler." Review of *Wintergreen*. *Sunday Olympian* (April 10, 1988).

Wellejus, Ed. "Butterfly." Review of *The Audubon Society Handbook for Butterfly Watchers*. *Erie (Pa.) Times* (August 6, 1984).

Wiese, William H. Review of *The Thunder Tree*. *Library Journal* 118, no. 7 (April 15, 1993).

Wiley, John P., Jr. Review of *IUCN Invertebrate Red Data Book*. *Smithsonian* 13, no. 5 (August 1983).

Wilkinson, Todd. "Bigfoot Lives!" *Profiles* (July 1995).

———. "'Hi, I'm Ted Koppel . . . and This . . . Is Bigfoot.'" Review of *Where Bigfoot Walks*. *Jackson Hole News* (May 24, 1995).

Wilson, Bob. Review of *Wintergreen*. *Audubon Warbler* (Portland Audubon Society) 51, no. 1 (January 1987). Reprinted in *Earthcare Northwest* (Seattle Audubon Society) 28, no. 7 (April 1987).

Winder, Robert. "Flights of Fancy." Review of *Nabakov's Butterflies*. *New Statesman* (April 10, 2000).

Winter, Dave. Review of *The Audubon Field Guide to North American Butterflies*. *News of the Lepidopterists' Society* (September/October 1981).

Winters, Matt. "Butterfly Power." *Chinook Observer* (August 25, 1999). Reprinted as "Gray's River Writer Wears Learning Lightly." Review of *Chasing Monarchs*. *Daily Astorian* (August 27, 1999).

———. "Lessons from a Wasteland." Review of *The Thunder Tree*. *Chinook Observer* (May 25, 1993).

Woldt, Arthur. Review of *Handbook for Butterfly Watchers*. *Conservationist* 47, no. 47 (February 1993).

Wurmstadt, Robert C. Review of *The Thunder Tree*. *The Warbler* (Denver Audubon Society) (1993).

ACKNOWLEDGMENTS FOR "WALKING THE HIGH RIDGE"

by Robert Michael Pyle

For including me in the *Credo* series and thus giving me this remarkable indulgence, I am especially grateful to Emilie Buchwald and Scott Slovic; and to them both again for their astute edits and Scott's kind profile. At Milkweed I also thank Laurie Buss, Beth Olson, Christine Baynes, and their collegues.

I owe thanks to the Sitka Center for Art and Ecology of Otis, Oregon, and its director Randall Koch, for refreshing retreats beneath the spruces that have meant much to this piece of work; and to Kim Stafford for inviting me there.

Any credo is a stew with many cooks. Everyone mentioned or quoted in these pages has helped me to make mine, and the life that goes with it. I mention especially my longtime editor at Houghton Mifflin, Harry Foster, a *sina qua non* if there ever was one; Fayette Krause and JoAnne Heron for their constant support; and Thea Linnaea Pyle, who shares the belief.

Of all the communities I have been privileged to belong to, three call for recognition here: the people of Gray's River, Washington; the writers and workers of the Orion Society, indigenous to the meeting ground between people and nature; and my local writing group: Brian Harrison, Susan Holway, John Indermark, Pat Thomas, Jenelle Varila, and Lorne Wirkkala.

And I thank Ed Maxwell immensely, for fixing Marsha.

WORKS CITED

p. viii   Vladimir Nabokov, "A World of
Butterflies," book review of *Audubon's
Butterflies, Moths, and Other Studies*,
edited by Alice Ford. *New York Times
Book Review* (December 28, 1952): 14.

p. 21   F. Martin Brown, Don Eff, and Bernard
Rotger, *Colorado Butterflies* (Denver:
Museum of Natural History, 1954), 29.

p. 30   Robert Michael Pyle, "Conservation and
Natural History," *Northwest Conifer*
(March 1968): 12.

p. 32   Jack Cady, *The American Writer* (New
York: St. Martin's Press, 1999), 261.

p. 48   Nabokov, "A World of Butterflies," 14.

p. 48   Nabokov, lecture on Charles Dickens's
Bleak House in *Lectures on Literature*

(New York: Harcourt Brace Jovanovich, 1980), 123.

p. 66   John Gardner, *On Becoming a Novelist* (New York: Harper and Row, 1983), 117.

p. 74   Pyle, *The Thunder Tree: Lessons from an Urban Wildland* (Boston: Houghton Mifflin, 1993), 147.

pp. 81–82   Pyle, *Where Bigfoot Walks* (Boston: Houghton Mifflin, 1995), 304–305.

p. 87   Robinson Jeffers, "Calm and Full the Ocean," in *Rock and Hawk* (New York: Random House, 1987), 234.

p. 88   Martin Amis, *The Information* (New York: Harmony, 1995), 329.

pp. 92–93   Pyle, *Wintergreen: Listening to the Land's Heart* (Boston: Houghton Mifflin, 1988), 273, 276, 277, 272, 274–75.

p. 94   Bruce Springsteen, "Badlands," on *Darkness on the Edge of Town* (New York: Columbia Records, 1978).

p. 97   Ann Zwinger, *The Nearsighted Naturalist* (Tucson: University of Arizona, 1998), 176.

p. 98   Alexander Skutch, *Life Ascending* (Austin: University of Texas Press, 1985), 258.

pp. 102–3 Charles Darwin, *The Origin of Species* (London: Oxford University Press, 1956), 560.

p. 104 Nabokov, *Speak, Memory* (New York: Putnam, 1966), 139.

p. 105 Jack Kerouac, *On the Road* (Mattituck, N.Y.: Amereon House, 1983), 95.

p. 105 Bruce Springsteen, "All That Heaven Will Allow," on *Tunnel of Love* (New York: Columbia Records, 1987).

p. 109 Herman Melville, *Moby-Dick* (New York: Modern Library, 1930), 207.

p. 115 Barbara Drake, "The Burnt Pot," in *What We Say to Strangers* (Portland: Breitenbush, 1986), 19.

p. 119 Harry Middleton, *The Earth Is Enough: Growing Up in a World of Trout and Old Men* (New York: Simon and Schuster, 1989).

p. 120 William Blake, "The Gates of Paradise," in *The Illuminated Blake,* annotated by David V. Erdman (Garden City, N.Y.: Anchor Press/Doubleday, 1974), 273.

pp. 121–22 Pyle, *Wintergreen: Listening to the Land's Heart* (Boston: Hougton Mifflin, 1995), 7.

p. 122 Pyle, *Wintergreen,* 303.

pp. 122–23 Pyle, *Wintergreen,* 100.

p. 124   Pyle, *Wintergreen,* 141.

p. 125   Janisse Ray, *Ecology of a Cracker Childhood* (Minneapolis: Milkweed Editions, 1999), 3.

pp. 125–26 Pyle, *Wintergreen,* 231–32.

pp. 126–27 Pyle, *Wintergreen,* 237–38.

pp. 127–28 Pyle, *Wintergreen,* 272–73.

p. 128   Pyle, *Wintergreen,* 273–74.

p. 128   Edward Abbey, *Desert Solitaire* (New York: Ballantine, 1971), 20.

p. 128   Pyle, *Wintergreen,* 277.

p. 129   Pyle, *Wintergeen,* 282.

p. 129   Pyle, *Wintergreen,* 293.

pp. 135–36 Roger Tory Peterson, Foreword, *Handbook for Butterfly Watchers,* by Robert Michael Pyle (Boston: Houghton Mifflin, 1992), xv–xvi.

p. 136   Ray Kelleher, "From a Distance, the Study of Butterflies Looks Like an Obsessive Pursuit of Nothing at All. On a Figurative Level, the Same Could Be Said of the Writing Life: An Interview with Robert Michael Pyle," *Poets &*

Writers Magazine 24, no. 2 (March/April 1996): 60.

p. 137   Jane Elder Wulff, "Dr. Robert Michael Pyle: A Meticulous Observer of Life," *Peninsula Magazine* 7, no. 3 (Fall 1992): 20.

p. 139   Pyle, *The Thunder Tree: Lessons from an Urban Wildland* (Boston: Houghton Mifflin, 1993), 146.

p. 140   Pyle, "Elegy Written in a Country Farmyard," *Illahee: Journal for the Northwest Environment* (Institute for Environmental Studies, University of Washington) (Fall/Winter 1995): 128.

pp. 140–41 Casey Walker, "An Interview with Robert Michael Pyle," *Wild Duck Review* (February 1997): 26.

p. 141   Faris Cassell, "Hearts All Aflutter: When Monarch Butterflies Take Wing, the Human Imagination Takes Flight," *Register-Guard* (Eugene, Oregon) (October 24, 1999): 5B.

pp. 142–43 Pyle, *The Thunder Tree,* 198.

SCOTT SLOVIC, founding president of the Association for the Study of Literature and Environment (ASLE), currently serves as editor of the journal *ISLE: Interdisciplinary Studies in Literature and Environment*. He is the author of *Seeking Awareness in American Nature Writing: Henry Thoreau, Annie Dillard, Edward Abbey, Wendell Berry, Barry Lopez* (University of Utah Press, 1992); his coedited books include *Being in the World: An Environmental Reader for Writers* (Macmillan, 1993), *Reading the Earth: New Directions in the Study of Literature and the Environment* (University of Idaho Press, 1998), and *Literature and the Environment: A Reader on Nature and Culture* (Addison Wesley Longman, 1999). Currently he is an associate professor of English and the director of the Center for Environmental Arts and Humanities at the University of Nevada, Reno.

MORE BOOKS ON
THE WORLD AS HOME
FROM MILKWEED EDITIONS

To order books or for more information,
contact Milkweed at (800) 520-6455
or visit our website (www.worldashome.org).

Brown Dog of the Yaak:
Essays on Art and Activism
Rick Bass

Boundary Waters:
The Grace of the Wild
Paul Gruchow

Grass Roots:
The Universe of Home
Paul Gruchow

The Necessity of Empty Places
Paul Gruchow

A Sense of the Morning:
Field Notes of a Born Observer
David Brendan Hopes

Taking Care:
Thoughts on Storytelling and Belief
William Kittredge

The Barn at the End of the World:
The Apprenticeship of a Quaker, Buddhist Shepherd
Mary Rose O'Reilley

Ecology of a Cracker Childhood
Janisse Ray

The Dream of the Marsh Wren:
Writing As Reciprocal Creation
Pattiann Rogers

The Country of Language
Scott Russell Sanders

Of Landscape and Longing:
Finding a Home at the Water's Edge
Carolyn Servid

The Book of the Tongass
Edited by Carolyn Servid and Donald Snow

Homestead
Annick Smith

Shaped by Wind and Water:
Reflections of a Naturalist
Ann Haymond Zwinger

Testimony:
Writers of the West Speak On Behalf of Utah Wilderness
Compiled by Stephen Trimble and
Terry Tempest Williams

OTHER BOOKS OF INTEREST TO
THE WORLD AS HOME READER:

Essays

*The Heart Can Be Filled Anywhere on Earth:
Minneota, Minnesota*
Bill Holm

*Shedding Life:
Disease, Politics, and Other Human Conditions*
Miroslav Holub

Children's novels

No Place
Kay Haugaard

The Monkey Thief
Aileen Kilgore Henderson

Treasure of Panther Peak
Aileen Kilgore Henderson

The Dog with Golden Eyes
Frances Wilbur

Anthologies

Sacred Ground:
Writings about Home
Edited by Barbara Bonner

Urban Nature:
Poems about Wildlife in the City
Edited by Laure-Anne Bosselaar

Verse and Universe:
Poems about Science and Mathematics
Edited by Kurt Brown

Poetry

Boxelder Bug Variations
Bill Holm

Butterfly Effect
Harry Humes

Eating Bread and Honey
Pattiann Rogers

Firekeeper:
New and Selected Poems
Pattiann Rogers

Typeset in Stone Serif
by Stanton Publication Services, Inc.
Printed on acid-free, recycled
55# Frasier Miami Book Natural paper
by Friesen Corporation.